PROFESSIONAL BOWLERS ASSOCIATION

GUIDE TO

BETTER BOWLING

Chuck Pezzano

SIMON AND SCHUSTER • NEW YORK

SBN 671-21627-9
Library of Congress Catalog Card Number: 73-18734
Designed by Irving Perkins
Manufactured in the United States of America

4   5   6   7   8   9   10

ACKNOWLEDGMENTS

A book is a team effort and we had a great team. Our thanks to Joe Antenora, executive director of the Professional Bowlers Association, and Eddie Elias, founder and legal counsel of the PBA, for their invaluable guidance. Thanks must go to Al Matzelle and Bruce Pluckhahn of the American Bowling Congress; Woody Woodruff, Al Spanjer and Mike Matera of AMF, Inc.; Milt Rudo and Art Serbo of Brunswick Corporation; and Bob Sicard of the Ebonite Corporation. Also to all those of the National Bowling Council who helped so graciously when asked.

Star bowlers are in a class by themselves, as shown by their willingness to share their hard-earned knowledge and ideas. We would have been lost without them.

And finally, our appreciation to Peter Schwed and Christine Steinmetz, a pair of word masters from Simon and Schuster, who acted as the quarterbacks and put it all together.

CONTENTS

1

INTRODUCTION

When the Professional Bowlers Association began its tournament tour in 1959, a new dimension was added to the field of bowling instruction. Prior to the advent of the PBA, a few major events were staged each year, but competitive bowling was a serious business to only a mere handful, who for the most part kept their bowling secrets to themselves.

Once the PBA tour solidified into more than thirty tournaments each year, it became increasingly evident that here was the storeroom of knowledge, the incubator of new techniques. Never before had so many experts of the game been assembled in the same place for so long a time.

The world's greatest bowlers, each with his own ideas, each with a chance to practice and test his ideas and theories under the most demanding competitive conditions, had found a home. They could compare notes with other pros and perform under the watchful eye of another pro dedicated to the same end, bowling perfection.

Pro bowlers now keep few secrets from each other, partly because they can't in many instances, but mostly because they have no desire to hold information back. If and when a pro comes up with something new, he usually can't wait to tell someone all about it.

It's the nature of the game. These men travel together, eat together, sleep in the same rooms. They know and savor the thrill of victory, and have sadly learned the agony of defeat.

On the lanes competing against each other, no quarter is asked, none given. It's really a lonely sort of sport, man against man, no team for support. And a pro bowler wants to win, not because his opponent bowls badly, but because they both rolled well, and he bowled just a little bit better.

Proof of the vast distribution of knowledge on the tour is the speedy development of so many young bowlers. They start at an early age, learn the basics and then go on tour. The young touring bowler learns more about the game in his first six months than the average bowler learns in ten years.

The following pages bring you the accumulated knowledge of more than one thousand of the world's greatest bowlers. You will find the names of the men who have made, are making and will make bowling history.

There is no one right way to bowl. There are fundamentals you must observe, in your own way, suited to your own body and your own mental makeup. The only real test of a system is whether it works or not. What you will read has worked. In addition, there are extra little tips from many of the bowlers, inside stuff that has helped put them on top.

But, as Hall of Famer Tony Sparando once put it, "It's great to be inexperienced enough to know everything. Trouble is that the older you get, the more there is to learn. And even when you're ready to quit, there's still much you haven't learned."

In reading this book you will find repetition. Key fundamentals cannot be emphasized too many times in one form or another. You may find some contradictions too, as there are areas where full agreement has not been reached and because bowling is such an individual game.

What is natural for one bowler might not be for another. This book is to be used as a guide. Hopefully it will answer all your bowling questions.

TONY SPARANDO

2

A SHORT HISTORY
OF BOWLING

Oddly, one of the babies of professional sports, bowling is also one of the most ancient sports. In one form or another, bowling has been around for more than seven thousand years. First traces were discovered in Egyptian tombs, but historians feel that the caveman may well have pursued his form of the sport, using rocks or pebbles to toss at other rocks or pebbles.

Though it's likely the game in some fashion was played by the Romans, Phoenicians and Carthaginians, no proof is available. We do know that in Julius Caesar's time, around 50 B.C., people in the Alpine regions of Italy played a game considered the precursor to "bocce," the Italian form of the game which is still played.

Bowling has been known by such names as bowls, skittles, kegling, nine-pins, Dutch pins and quilles.

The word *bowl* could be derived from the Saxon *bolla* and Danish *bolle* which meant "bubble" originally, but which later came to mean anything spherical. Then again, it may be from the Latin *bulla* or the old French *boule,* both meaning "ball." One thing is sure—the word *bowl* or its equivalent is to be found in all languages of the Teutonic group.

According to ancient records, Germany's first bowling took on a religious significance. In the early Christian era citizens carried staves or clubs called kegles or kegels. They were used for many purposes, from beating through bushes to beating off attackers.

BOWLING ON THE GREEN IN COLONIAL DAYS.

But in the cathedral cloisters the kegle was set up to represent the devil. The citizen was then given a rock or some sort of ball and asked to hit the kegle. If he scored a hit, his life was clean; he had proved it by knocking off the devil. If he missed, it indicated his aim needed improvement, and maybe more faithful churchgoing was the answer.

The users of the kegle were called keglers, a term still widely used to describe bowlers. Or so that story goes.

The game was supposedly so popular in fourteenth-century England that the young men were skipping archery in favor of bowling. King Edward III passed a law to stop all that nonsense. Other kings had bowling banned because it became a popular gambling sport.

Popular it was, for in 1455 the sport that had been an outdoor game was brought under a roof for the first time so a game wouldn't be called because of rain.

One of the favorite historical tales of bowling concerns Sir Francis Drake, who didn't stop bowling even though his scouts informed him that the Spanish Armada was approaching in strike formation. Admiral Drake

insisted there was time to score some of his own strikes and still strike down the Spaniards. He did.

All types of bowling games flourished in various parts of the world, including lawn bowling in England and the Irish road bowling, a game in which bowlers rolled stones on ice. Pins in various numbers, shapes and forms were used. Martin Luther was usually too busy to bowl himself but history records that he went so far as to construct a lane for his family since he considered it good family recreation. The Scotch refined the game, put it on a high plane.

Bowling came to the New World in the 1600s as the game of ninepins, a favorite of the early Dutch explorers and settlers who came to the northeastern section of the United States. It became very popular with the early Dutch and German people, and even the Puritans found the game to their liking, despite their consistent objection to anything that might possibly bring pleasure.

The game of ninepins was a popular betting game, too popular for some lawmakers, who outlawed the game. One of the great heroes of sports history, whose name unfortunately is unknown, circumvented the law by adding the tenth pin. This changed the entire game for the better in every way, and bowling was on its way to respectability.

There were various groups in bowling, most doing more fighting than bowling. But in 1895 the best men in these groups got together to form the American Bowling Congress.

Since then, the ABC, a nonprofit organization of male tenpin bowlers, has established playing rules, set equipment standards and specifications and promoted bowling as a wholesome recreation and exciting competitive sport.

From a few hundred league bowlers in 1895 the ABC now sanctions some 4 million male bowlers and 10,000 tournaments, and certifies more than 140,000 lanes in 10,000 bowling centers.

Women bowlers are vital to the game. The distaffers organized the

ABE LINCOLN BOWLED IN LEISURE TIME.

EX-PRESIDENT NIXON HAS ALWAYS BEEN AN AVID BOWLER.

Women's International Bowling Congress in 1916 with some 40 members. That total has now surpassed 3 million. In 1972 more than 50 million people bowled.

Thanks to the ABC and the WIBC, the rules of the game are well defined for all. Everyone can compete with everyone else because the lanes, balls, and rules are standardized and many systems of handicapping have been developed.

Hundreds of thousands of volunteer workers aid in keeping bowling popular. It is one of the most organized sports of all. Each segment cooperates through the National Bowling Council.

Bowling received its greatest boost with the advent of the automatic pinspotter. It was a big step in allowing the businessman of the game, the bowling center owner, to remodernize both his center and his thinking. Bowling became a complete family sport, with modern, efficient equipment available at all times for men, women and children.

In practically all surveys taken in the early 1970s, bowling had reached the point where it rated only behind football, baseball and basketball, not only as the most popular sport but as the sport people like to follow most. Bowling has long been the number one participant sport.

There are bowling lanes in the basements of private homes, in the most public home of all, the White House, in castles in Europe and in ships at sea as well as in the Playboy Mansion. So it's easy to see that bowling reaches a wide range of people and places.

3

PROFESSIONAL BOWLING

Some areas of bowling history are obscure, shrouded in doubt and still wide open to argument and speculation. One fact of bowling is crystal clear: Eddie Elias is the father of professional bowling.

There were professional bowlers long before Elias was born in 1928. Prior to the turn of the century some of the better bowlers were called on to demonstrate new balls and new grips. But these were one-shot deals. Hall of Famer Jimmy Smith toured the nation as an exhibition bowler from 1910 through 1924. He is generally considered the first professional bowler.

EDDIE ELIAS, FOUNDER OF PBA.

ANDY VARIPAPA, EARLY PRO, STILL ACTIVE INTO HIS EIGHTIES.

It wasn't too much later that Andy Varipapa came along. His forte was showmanship and it led to lucrative tours for him and stardom in the first movie short about bowling in 1934.

Groups of bowling proprietors and manufacturers did use bowlers from time to time to sell both the game of bowling and its products, but the opportunities were few and far between for the most part. A star bowler, unless he was a Smith or a Varipapa, could never make a living at the game. And in Varipapa's case, he always vigorously promoted himself and hired agents to set up his tours.

There were only a few major tournaments: the annual ABC tournament, and later on the All-Star, started in 1941, plus a few other outstanding events such as the Petersen Classic, where a bowler could win a hefty cash prize. For the most part, the better bowlers made their own action by rolling against each other for huge bets. This was more an ego matter, an attempt to determine who was best, than a way to make a living.

It was after World War II when bowling increased in popularity and new bowling centers were constructed in huge numbers, that the so-called pro started to earn real money. In the 1950s there were probably more than fifty bowlers making a living or good part-time income rolling at grand openings, reopenings and the like. Some of the big names had contracts with the manufacturers and also with commercial sponsors.

From time to time attempts had been made to form some sort of professional group, basically to set standard fees for appearances, both on the lanes and off, and to come up with a set of rules to determine what tournaments they should or would roll in. Trial balloons never got far off the ground.

It was in 1958 after much spadework that Elias, a young lawyer with a dream, turned preacher to outline the potential of his dream to a group of top bowlers who were in Syracuse for another tournament. Most of the bowlers, and most of the bowling industry, took a wait-and-see attitude.

Thirty-three bowlers heard more than a wild dream in the words coming from the big man with the dark hair and the big eyes. And the thirty-three men put up fifty dollars apiece, their bet that this man would do what no other had been able to do in the past.

He promised opportunity more than anything else. In his plans he outlined a tournament tour, an insurance program, TV shows, endorsements and a position in the sports world for the bowler as an athlete.

It wasn't easy, but he did it. The big money purses that now give any youngster a chance at a career are only part of the Elias story. The Elias influence made professionals out of semipros. It made members walk, talk and think like pros. He took the top names of the game—Carter, Weber, Welu and the like—and put them into an imaginative concept that has appealed to the entire national public, kids and oldsters, bowlers and even nonbowlers.

Even lesser lights among PBA members have fared well. These days a pro knows that if he buckles down, works hard and, most important, bowls well, rewards that have come to Carter and Weber and others (annual incomes of more than $100,000) can be his too.

Eddie Elias worked out the dream for a professional group and brought it off.

THE PBA STORY

1958 • Eddie Elias, Akron, Ohio, attorney, founded the PBA. There were 33 charter members.

1959 • The PBA tournament tour got off to a halting start with three tournaments worth $49,500. The first of many television shows was inaugurated with "Jackpot Bowling."

1960 • Seven tournaments worth $150,000 went into the record book. "Make That Spare" poured more television money into PBA members' pockets. A $5,000 life insurance plan went into effect.

1961 • Eleven tournaments worth $250,000. The first televised show of a PBA finals was instigated in the $75,000 National PBA Invitational at Paramus, N.J.

1962 • Thirty-two tournaments worth $800,000. The winter tour finals went on the air for the first time. This was the opening of a series which was still running in 1973 on ABC-TV.

1963 • Thirty-eight tournaments, worth $1,000,000. "Make That Spare" was still going strong and Don Carter made history when he broke the jackpot.

1964 • Thirty-one tournaments worth $1,200,000. The PBA put another television show on the air, the two-man bestball over CBS-TV.

1965 • Thirty-two tournaments worth $1,300,000. Elias negotiated for the biggest tournament in the history of the game, the $100,000 Firestone Tournament of Champions at Akron, Ohio, home of the PBA. Elias also formed the Image Committee.

1966 • Twenty-nine tournaments worth $1,500,000. Wayne Zahn earned $54,720 to break Don Carter's mark of $49,972 established in 1962. Membership grew from 33 to 900. The PBA held a tournament in Caracas, Venezuela. Steve Nagy passed away.

1967 • Thirty-four tournaments worth $1,600,000. The PBA started two new bureaus for its membership: the Job Placement Bureau and the Exhibition Bureau. Ebonite became a tournament sponsor along with Brut. Miller had been in one year, which, along with Firestone, raised the total of commercial sponsors to four. The PBA went into the new Madison Square Garden for the $70,000 National Championship.

1969 • Thirty-five tournaments worth $1,800,000. This was the eighth straight year the winter tour was on ABC-TV. American Airlines and Bellows-Valvair joined as major tournament sponsors, and Billy Hardwick set a new record by winning seven tournaments during the year. The first National Resident Professional Championship was held at Cincinnati.

1970 • Prize money continued upward and for the ninth straight year the ABC television network carried the finals of the PBA winter tour. The PBA's twelfth year saw the regional tournament program catch on, with 26 events. The Don Carter Classic was new. Bellows-Valvair cosponsored four tournaments, while Firestone, Miller High Life, Lincoln-Mercury, Ebonite and American Airlines continued their major events.

1971 • A winter tour that approached the $1,000,000 mark and an expanded regional program marked the PBA's thirteenth year. New sponsors were the R. J. Reynolds Tobacco Co. and Andy Granatelli's STP organization. Washington, D.C., hosted an event, while Lincoln-Mercury and Madison Square Garden joined to stage the Cougar Open. ABC-TV and the PBA celebrated their tenth year together, and Don Johnson and Johnny Petraglia waged a pitched battle for top honors.

1972 • A more lucrative season than ever before and an important factor was the new price tag—$125,000—given to the Firestone Tournament of Champions. Madison Square Garden was to host the BPAA

U.S. Open as the season opener, the Ebonite Open was to shift to Miami, Fla., and the Cougar was slated for San Jose, Calif., while Andy Granatelli moved his STP Classic to New Orleans. PBA membership was expected to hit an all-time high.

1973 • Another rise in total prize money to $2,300,000. Regional activities increased with more than 40 tournaments. Big controversy over soaking of bowling balls with chemicals ended when both PBA and ABC banned such practices. Don McCune came into his own after many years as just another pro. Cable TV aired 10 tournaments.

1974 • The PBA signed a three-year contract with ABC-TV to air the winter tour through 1977, making it sixteen years in a row for the telecasts, second longest running sports show on TV. CBS also aired two tournaments and Home Box Office ten, so 26 tournaments were televised. Prize money rose to $2,500,000, and PBA membership reached an all-time high of more than 1,200. The PBA Hall of Fame was instituted. Projection for 1975 is prize money nearing the $3,000,000 mark.

1975 • PBA membership passed the 1,300 mark for the first time and prize money reached a record $2,700,000 despite the poor business climate and a lessening enthusiasm for sports sponsorships. Eighteen of 35 tournaments were nationally televised by ABC and CBS and the high ratings continued to amaze experts. An additional nine events were telecast regionally. Regional activity zoomed to more than 80 tournaments.

4

THE BOWLER'S DICTIONARY

Bowlers have a language all their own. Following is the most complete and up-to-date dictionary of the words of bowling. Some of the terms are seldom used, but most are in general usage. A simple reading will immediately upgrade your knowledge of bowling, add to your understanding of instructional phrases and tune you in closer to the pro side of the game.

A

ABC—American Bowling Congress, world's largest sports participation organization, official rule-making body of tenpin bowling.

AJBC—American Junior Bowling Congress.

Alley—Playing surface, made of maple and pine boards.

All the way—Means finishing a game from any point with nothing but strikes.

Anchor—Last man to roll in team competition.

Apple—Bowling ball. Also applied to bowler who fails to come through in a clutch situation.

Approach—Same as "runway."

Arrows—Aiming points embedded in the lane.

B

Baby the ball—Too delicate, not enough emphasis on delivering the ball with authority.

Baby split—The 2–7 or 3–10 split leave.

Baby split with company—The 2–7–8 or 3–9–10 split leave.

Backup—A ball that falls away to the right for right-handed bowlers, to the left for lefties.

Backup alley—A lane that holds or tends to stop a ball from rolling to the right.

Balk—An incomplete approach in which the bowler does not deliver the ball. To interfere or cause another bowler to stop his approach or not complete it in his normal fashion.

Ball rack—Where the ball rests before it is rolled and after it returns from the pit. Also the structure used to store house balls.

Ball track—Area of lane where most balls are rolled.

Barmaid—A pin hidden behind another pin.

Bed—The alley bed, synonymous with a single lane.

Bedposts—The 7–10 split.

Beer frame—In team play, when all but one of the players scores a strike, the one who doesn't must treat. Also any designated frame in which the bowler who scores the least must pick up a refreshment tab, usually liquid.

Belly the ball—Increase the width of a hook from an inside starting angle.

Bench work, bench jockeying—Any type of conversation or other actions intended to upset an opponent.

Bicycle—Hidden pin, same as "barmaid."

Big ball—A working hook that enables a bowler to carry strikes on something less than perfect pocket hits.

Big ears—The 4–6–7–10.

Big fill—Nine or 10 pins on a spare or on a double strike.

Big five—Spare leave of three on one side and two on the other.

Big four—The 4–6–7–10, same as "big ears."

Blind—Score allowed for absent member, usually low, as a penalty.

Blocked—A lane maintenance condition in which oil or some sort of lane finish is used to create a track.

Blow—A missed spare.

Blow a rack—A solid strike hit.

Blowout—Downing all the pins but one.

Board—A lane consists of individual strips of lumber called boards. Pros call them by number, fifth board, fifteenth board, etc., for targeting purposes.

Body english—Contortion of the arms, legs and trunk in an attempt to steer the ball after it has left the hand.

Bolsa—Same as "thin hit."

Bonus—In match play bowling, pins awarded for winning game, usually 30 or 50.

Box—Frame.

BPAA—Bowling Proprietors Association of America. Trade organization of the people who own bowling centers.

Break—A lucky shot. Also a stopper after a number of consecutive strikes.

Bridge—Distance separating finger holes.

Brooklyn—Left of headpin for a right-handed bowler.

Broom ball—A ball that hits the 1–3 pocket in such a way that the pins scatter as though they were swept with a broom.

Bucket—The 2–4–5–8 spare leave for righty; 3–5–6–9 for lefty.

C

CC—Double century or a 200 game.

Channel—Depression to right and left of lane to guide ball to pit should it leave the playing surface on the way down.

Charge—Term used by pros to describe a sensational spurt of high scoring.

Cheese cakes—Lanes on which strikes come easy.

Cherry—Chopping the front pin of a spare leave while a pin behind and/or to the left or right remains standing.

Choke—Fail to accomplish objective because of nervousness or fright. Same as "apple." Also cutting arm swing short.

Chop—Same as "cherry."

Christmas tree—The 3–7–10 leave for a righty or 2–7–10 for a lefty.

Cincinnati—The 8–10 split.

Classified—Leagues or tournaments with average limitations.

Clean game—Strike or spare in each of the ten frames.

Clothes line—The 1–2–4–7 or 1–3–6–10 spare leave.

Clutch—Pressure situation.

Count—Number of pins knocked down on first ball of each frame.

Cranker—Bowler who uses cranking motion to roll wide hook ball.

Creeper—Slow ball.

Crooked arm—Hook ball bowler who bends his elbow.

Cross—Going to the left side for a righty. Same as "Brooklyn."

Crow hopper—Loose, clawlike grip on ball at release point.

Curtain—Anchor man missing in final frame when a spare would have won for his team.

Curve—Ball that breaks from right to left (for righty) in a huge arc.

Cushion—Padding at rear of pit to absorb shock of ball and pins.

Cutter—Sharp-breaking hook which seems to slice the pins down.

D

Dead apple, dead ball—Ineffective ball, usually fades or deflects badly when it hits the pins.

Dead wood—Pins knocked down but remaining on the lane or in the gutter. Must be removed before continuing play.

Deflection—The movement of the ball when it comes into contact with the pins.

Dime store—The 5–10 split.

Dinner bucket, dinner pail—Same as "bucket."

Dive—The action of a ball that hooks greatly at the last split second.

Division boards—Where the pine and maple meet on a lane.

Dodo—A bowling ball over the legal weight or out of proper balance.

Double—Two strikes in a row.

Double pinochle—The 4–6–7–10 split, same as "big ears," "big four."

Double wood—Any two pins, when one is directly behind the other, the 1–5, 2–8 and 3–9.

Dovetails—Area of lane where maple and pine boards join. Also called "splice."

Drive—Another name for alley or lane. Also the revolving action of a ball as it contacts the pins.

Dummy—Same as "blind."

Dutch 200—A 200 game scored by alternating strikes and spares.

E

Emblem—The logo on a bowling ball, usually signifying the heaviest part of the ball.

Error—A miss. Same as "blow."

F

Faith, Hope, Charity—The 2–7–10 or 3–7–10 split, same as Christmas tree.

Fast—In different sections of the country the meaning is exactly the opposite. In one area it means a lane that allows a ball to hook easily, while in another area it means a lane that holds down the hook.

Fence posts—The 7–10 split.

Field goal—Ball rolled between two pins of a wide split.

Fill—Pins knocked down following a spare.

Fit split—Any split when it's possible for the ball to hit both pins.

Flat alley—A lane that despite perfect levelness doesn't run or hold with respect to the action of the ball.

Flat arc—The curved path of a ball in process of delivery when it is too low to the approach or off to either side and so not part of a perfect circle.

Flat ball—Ineffective ball, few revolutions, little action.

Floater—A ball that goes where the lane lets it. A ball released badly with no particular lift or turn.

Foul—Touching or going beyond the foul line at delivery.

Foul line—The marking that determines the beginning of the lane.

Foundation—A strike in the ninth frame.

Foundation, early—A strike in the eighth frame.

Frame—A tenth part of a game of bowling.

Frozen rope—A ball rolled with excessive speed almost straight into the pocket.

Fudge—Decrease revolutions on ball.

Full hit—A ball striking near the center of the headpin on a strike attempt or the middle of any pin you may be aiming at.

Full roller—A ball that rolls over its full circumference.

G

Getting the wood—A better than average score. Also making sure you take one pin down on an almost impossible split.

Goal posts—The 7–10 split. Same as "bedposts," "fence posts."

Golden gate—The 4–6–7–10 split. Same as "double pinochle," "big ears," "big four."

Grab—Means the friction between the lane and the ball is good, causing a sudden hook.

Grasshopper—An effective ball, particularly on light pocket hits.

Graveyards—Low-scoring lanes. In a high-scoring center applied to the lowest scoring pair of lanes.

Groove—Ball track or indentation in lane. Also applied to bowler who is performing well and has his approach and arm swing almost mechanically perfect.

Gutter—Same as "channel."

Gutter ball—A ball that goes into the gutter.

H

Half hit—Midway between a full hit and a light hit.

Handicap—Pins awarded to individuals or teams in an attempt to equalize competition.

Hard way—Rolling 200 by alternating strikes and spares. Same as "Dutch 200."

High board—Due to atmospheric conditions a board in a lane may expand or contract a tiny bit, but enough to change the course of a bowling ball should the ball roll in that area. Most boards contract leaving a low area or a low board, but it is still mistermed as a high board.

High hit—Ball contacting a pin near its center.

Higher—More to the left.

Hold, holding alley—A lane that resists hook action of a ball.

Hole—The 1–3 pocket, 1–2 for lefties. Also another name for "split."

Home alley—Favorite lane or pair of lanes for individuals or teams.

Honey—A good ball.

Hook—A ball that breaks to the left.

Hook alley—A lane on which the ball will move to the left easily.

Hot—When a bowler or team starts lining up strikes.

House ball—Bowling ball provided by center.

I

Inside—A starting point near the center of the lane as opposed to the outside, near the edge of the lane.

In there—A good pocket hit.

J

Jack Manders—Rolling through the middle of a 7–10 or any wide split. Same as "field goal."

Jam—Force the ball high into the pocket.

Jersey side—To the left of the headpin.

K

Kickback—Vertical division boards between lanes at the pit end. On many hits the pins bounce from the kickback knocking additional pins down.

Kick off—Smooth, effective ball delivery.

Kindling wood—Light pins.

Kingpin—The headpin or the number 5 pin, varying with local usage.

Kitty—Money collected from team members for misses, low games, and other set fines. Used to defray expenses in tournaments or divided equally at end of season.

Kresge—Whereas the 5–10 split is called the Woolworth, the 5–7 is often called the Kresge.

L

Lane—Playing surface. Same as "alley."

Late 10—When the 10 pin hesitates, and is the last to go down on a strike.

Leadoff—First man in a team lineup.

Lift—Means giving the ball upward motion with the fingers at the point of release.

Light—Not full on the target pin, too much to the right.

Lily—The 5–7–10 split.

Line—The path a bowling ball takes. Also one game of bowling.

Loafing—Not lifting or turning the ball properly, with the result that the ball lags and doesn't reach the target, usually rolling off to the right.

Lofting—Throwing the ball well out on the lane rather than rolling it.

Looper—An extra-wide hook ball, usually slow.

Loose hit—A light pocket hit which gives good pin action off the kickback.

Low—Light or thin hit on the headpin, as opposed to a high hit.

M

Maples—Pins.

Mark—A strike or spare.

Match play—Portion of tournament in which bowlers are pitted individually against each other.

Medal play—Strictly total pin scores.

Miss—An error or blow.

Mixer—Ball with action causing the pins to bounce around.

Mother-in-law—The 7 pin.

Move in—To start from or near center of approach.

Move out—To start from or near corner position on approach.

Mule ears—The 7–10 split.

Murphy—Baby split.

N

Nose hit—A first ball full on the headpin.

Nothing ball—Ineffective ball.

NBC—National Bowling Council.

O

One in the dark—Rear pin in the 1–5, 2–8 or 3–9 spare.

Open—A frame that doesn't produce a strike or spare.

Open bowling—Nonleague or nontournament play, for fun or practice.

Out and in—A wide hook rolled from the center of the lane toward the gutter; the ball hooks back to the pocket—going out, then in.

Outside—Corner or near corner position of playing lanes.

Over—in professional bowling scoring a 200 average is used as par. The number of pins above the 200 average is the number of pins over or in the black.

Over turn—To apply too much spin to the ball and not enough finger lift.

P

Pack—A full count of ten.

Part of the building—Expression referring to 7, 8 or 10 pin when it stands after what seems to be a perfect hit.

PBA—Professional Bowlers Association.

Pick—To knock down only the front pin from a spare leave. Same as "cherry" or "chop."

Pie alley—A lane that is easy to score on.

Pinching the ball—Gripping the ball too hard.

Pine—Softer wood used beyond division boards, takes over where maple ends.

Pit—Space at end of lane where ball and pins wind up.

Pitch—Angle at which holes in bowling ball are drilled.

Pocket—The 1–3 for righties, 1–2 for lefties.

Point—To aim more directly at the pocket, high and tight.

Poison ivy—The 3–6–10.

Poodle—To roll a gutter ball.

Position rounds—Designated parts of a league or tournament schedule which call for teams or players to meet each other based on their standings. First place meets second, third meets fourth, fifth meets sixth, etc.

Pot game—Competition in which two or more bowlers post some sort of stake and high man takes it all.

Powder puff, puff ball—Slow ball that fails to carry the pins.

Powerhouse—A hard, strong ball for a strike, carrying all ten pins into the pit.

Puddle—A gutter ball.

Pumpkin—Bowling ball that hits soft.

Punch out—Strike out.

Q

Quick eight—A good pocket hit which leaves the 4–7 for righties, 6–10 for lefties.

R

Railroad—Better known as "split."

Rap—When a single pin remains standing on a good hit.

Rat club—A team shooting horribly low scores for one game.

Reading the lanes—Discovering whether a lane hooks or holds, and where the best place is to roll the ball to score high.

Return—The track on which balls roll from pit to ball rack.

Reverse—An emphatic backup.

Revolutions—The turns a ball takes to go from the foul line to the pins.

Run, running lane—A lane on which the ball hooks easily.

Runway—Starting area. Also known as platform, approach. Ends at the foul line, where the lane starts.

S

Sandbagger—Bowler who keeps his average down purposely in order to receive a higher handicap than he deserves.

Sandwich game—Same as "Dutch 200."

Scenic route—Path taken by big curve ball.

Schleifer—Thin-hit strike where pins seem to fall one by one.

Scratch—Rolling without benefit of handicap. Actual score.

Set—Ball holding in the pocket.

Short pin—A pin rolling on the alley bed which just fails to reach and hit a standing pin.

Shotgun shot—Rolling the ball from the hip.

Sidearming—Allowing the arm to draw away from its proper position during back and forward swing.

Sleeper—A pin hidden behind another pin.

Slick—Lane condition highly polished, tends to hold back hook.

Slot alley—Lane on which strikes come easy.

Small ball—Type of ball that doesn't mix the pins, must hit pocket perfectly for strikes.

Snake eyes—The 7–10 split.

Snow plow—A ball that clears all the pins for a strike.

Soft alley—A lane on which strikes come easy.

Sour apple—Weak ball, one that leaves the 5–7, 5–10 or 5–7–10 split.

Span—Distance between thumb and finger holes.

Spare—All pins down with two balls.

Spare leave—Refers to pins standing after first ball is rolled.

Spiller—A light-hit strike in which the pins seem to melt away, taking a longer time than other type strikes.

Splasher—A strike where the pins are downed quickly.

Splice—Where maple and pine boards join on the lane.

Split—A spare leave in which the headpin is down and the remaining combination of pins have an intermediate pin down immediately ahead of or between them.

Spot—Target on lane at which the bowler aims, could be a dot, a dark board or an arrow.

Steal—Get more pins than you deserve on a strike hit.

Stiff alley—A lane with a tendency to hold a hook ball back.

Strap the ball—Get maximum lift.

Strike—All ten pins down on the first ball.

Strike out—Finish the game with strikes.

Strike split—The 8–10. Ball looks like a good strike ball, but leaves the split.

String—A number of continuous strikes. Also, in some areas, one game of bowling.

Sweeper—A wide-breaking hook which carries a strike as though the pins were pushed with a broom.

Sweepstakes—Bowling tournament.

T

Tandem—Two pins, one behind the other.

Tap—When a pin stands on an apparently perfect hit.

Telephone poles—Heavy pins.

Thin hit—A pocket hit when the ball barely touches the headpin.

Three quarters—Spot where bowlers place ball upon delivery, midway between right corner and center of lane and three fourths of the width of the lane from the left corner. A popular starting point.

Throwing rocks—Piling up strikes with a speed ball.

Topping the ball—At ball release when fingers are on top of the ball instead of behind or to the side. Causes a bad ball with little action.

Touch—Pin standing on a good hit.

Tripped 4—When the 2 pin takes out the 4 pin by bouncing off the kickback.

Turkey—Three strikes in a row.

Turn—Motion of hand toward pocket area at point of ball release.

U

Umbrella ball—A high hit on the nose resulting in a strike.

Under—In professional bowling scoring, a 200 average is used as par. The number of pins below the 200 average is the number of pins the bowler is under or in the red.

Up the hill—Refers to coaxing a ball over a high board into the pocket.

V

Venting—Drilling a small hole (not a finger hole) to relieve suction in the thumb hole.

W

Washout—The 1–2–10 or 1–2–4–10 leave.

Water in the ball—A weak ball, one that leaves an 8–10, 5–7 or 5–10.

WIBC—Women's International Bowling Congress.

Winding them in—Refers to big-hook-ball bowlers who get their hooks around the pocket consistently.

Wood—(a) In handicapping, the number of pins given. ("How much wood will you give me?")
(b) In scoring, number of pins knocked down. ("He didn't get all the wood.")

Wooden bottles—Pins.

Woolworth—The 5–10 split.

Working ball—A ball with enough action to mix the pins on an offpocket hit and have them scramble each other for a strike. The same ball will break up splits when it hits the nose.

X

X—Symbol for strike.

Y

Yank the shot—When a bowler hangs on to the ball too long and pulls it across his body.

Z

Zero in—Find the right strike spot on a lane.

5

EQUIPMENT

BOWLING BALLS, FITS AND GRIPS

From the beginning of time people have thrown things at other things, including each other. This natural action leads to the assumption that rocks were probably the first bowling balls used. That first bowler would be amazed to see the finely honed, precision product today's bowler rolls down the lanes.

The first real bowling balls were made of lignum vitae, a tropical wood so dense it won't float in water. It is often referred to as "ironwood."

Wooden bowling balls were hardly the ideal. They chipped and cracked and several months of banging away at the pins or any exposure to extremes of heat or cold did odd things to their shape. A quick trip to the manufacturer made the ball round again, but also smaller. In turning the ball down on the lathe, some of the wood had to be worn away.

Originally, bowling balls were palmed, held in the center of the hand much the same as duckpin and candlepin balls are held today. A good bowler developed enough control to roll the ball straight or impart a hook.

No one knows exactly when finger holes appeared, but as the game of tenpins standardized, using the triangular setup of ten pins, with each pin's center 12 inches from the nearest pin's center, the size of the ball increased.

The men who founded the American Bowling Congress in 1895 decided the ball should not exceed 27 inches in circumference. Every bowler

THE TWO-FINGERED GRIP FOR BOWLING BALLS WAS INTRODUCED IN THE UNITED STATES IN THE 1880s. PRIOR TO THAT TIME BOWLERS PALMED THE BOWLING SPHERES. BRUNSWICK'S FAMOUS MINERALITE BALL WAS PLACED ON THE MARKET IN 1906.

wanted to use the largest ball possible, and since it wasn't easy to palm the large ball, the almost obvious solution was to place holes in the ball.

Though used previously, finger holes gained widespread acceptability in the 1898–99 season. An all-star team toured to demonstrate the new innovation and helped make finger holes so popular that shortly after the turn of the century finger holes were standard.

Early bowling balls had only two holes, one for the middle finger and one for the thumb. This practice remained in vogue until the end of World War I. Then it became increasingly evident to the scoffers that three holes, adding a hole for the ring finger, allowed a better grip, enabled the bowler to roll more games with less strain, and gave the bowler the option of various types of grip.

Though the size of the bowling ball had been determined in 1895, the American Bowling Congress had no weight specifications until 1903. In that year convention delegates limited the weight to sixteen and a half pounds. The weight restriction met with great opposition from bowling clubs across the nation.

In 1904 the delegates quelled the uproar when they voted to allow each city association to regulate bowling ball weights in its own territory. That didn't work too well, and in 1905 the ABC again came up with a weight restriction in its bowling ball specifications. The 16-pound weight adopted remains the standard today.

How did the bowling pioneers arrive at the size of the ball? Early bowlers took pride in the game. They were leaders in their communities, and were well versed in science and math. They agreed, after much study and discussion, that placing 10 pins in a triangle, spaced 12 inches apart, with the headpin 60 feet from the foul line made an interesting, exciting and skillful game.

The size of the ball was vital. Too big and it would detract from the skill needed. Too small and the game would become too difficult. A ball 27 inches in circumference or less proved to be the answer. A ball that size could topple two parallel pins such as the 4–5 and 5–6, if the bowler behind the ball was skillful enough to fit the ball between.

Next in the evolution of the bowling ball came the search to find a substitute for lignum vitae. In 1905 came the announcement of the "Indestructible Hard Rubber Ball," developed and manufactured by the American Hard Rubber Company of New York. The hard rubber ball ruled supreme for more than half a century, until 1960 when the ABC approved the use of plastics in the manufacture of bowling balls. This opened the door to a whole new world of colors, including clear, see-through models.

A bowling ball could well be the best investment in the sporting goods field. Made of hard rubber or plastics, such as epoxy and polyester, most are guaranteed for life. They usually outlast their owners and a generation or two beyond. Every bowling ball manufacturer—and there are dozens throughout the world—is constantly looking to improve the bowling ball by coming as close to ABC specifications as possible in regard to roundness, weight and balance.

The shells (outer coating) of bowling balls made by different manufacturers vary in hardness. The pro bowler uses this fact to his advantage. The harder the finish, the more the ball will skid. The softer-shelled ball grips the lane more quickly and more effectively. If your ball hooks too much, a harder ball will help alleviate the problem. If your hook is on the weak side, a softer ball will help.

The average bowler doesn't know, and isn't expected to know, what a certain bowling ball will do because of the hardness or softness of the shell. A qualified professional at a pro shop knows the degrees of hardness of the various bowling balls and can determine what is best for each bowler.

A pro also knows about the weight of bowling balls. As mentioned previously, the weight limit is 16 pounds. For years the better bowlers, both men and women, insisted on a bowling ball of maximum allowable weight, and most preached that theory to other bowlers.

The pro tour proved that it's much more important to have a ball that fits properly, and that bowlers should use a ball they can handle easily, even at the sacrifice of some of the allowable weight.

Bill Bunetta, Hall of Famer, and one of the finest instructors in the game, experimented with bowling balls as light as 13 pounds.

"I had great success with high pocket hits and light pocket hits. The so-called half hit didn't work well because on this type of hit there is the most destructive deflection. However, I would not hesitate to recommend a lighter ball for almost any bowler."

Don Carter, named the greatest bowler of all time, and always a shining example of strength physically and mentally, feels that one of the great fallacies in bowling is the thinking in some quarters that a man isn't a man unless he uses a 16-pound ball.

"That's so silly," says Carter. "Probably half the male bowlers in the country would be more effective with a lighter ball. I've used as low as a fourteen and a half pounder and rolled well. Don't let pride rule common sense."

Dave Davis, a stringbean lefty who is one of pro bowling's all-time leading money winners, has used a light ball on and off for years. "I can swing it better and it gives me a chance to speed up a lot easier when I must," says the former Bowler of the Year. "I feel I don't lose a thing when I go to a lighter ball."

So the general consensus of all pros is that if you can use a 16-pound ball and it doesn't bother you or your game, fine. But don't ever hesitate to drop the weight if a lighter weight will give you more balance and coordination.

Moving into the drilling of a bowling ball, you will find that there are

BILL BUNETTA

DAVE DAVIS

as many grips as there are bowlers, and that's as it should be. Every hand is different. Every finger and thumb is different. Skin and flesh vary greatly in elasticity. So it's important, imperative actually, that every bowler seriously interested in bowling has his or her own bowling ball.

Sure, there are "house" balls in every bowling center. They are fine for the casual bowler. There is enough variety in the way they are drilled that almost everyone can find an approximate fit. And yet, in reality, they fit nobody. At the first opportunity, even if you intend to roll just now and then, obtain your own private bowling ball.

All ball drillings are offshoots of the three basic grips—conventional, semifingertip and full fingertip. Bowling balls and the drilling of them have created a language in itself. As these terms are important, it's necessary to have a working knowledge of them.

The *span* of a bowling ball is the distance from the inner edge of the thumb hole to the inner edge of the finger holes.

Pitch is the angle at which the hole is drilled into the ball with relationship to the center of the ball. Four basic pitches are used. *Forward pitch* is when the center line of the hole is angled toward the center of the ball. *Reverse pitch* is the result of the center line of the hole being drilled away from the center of the ball.

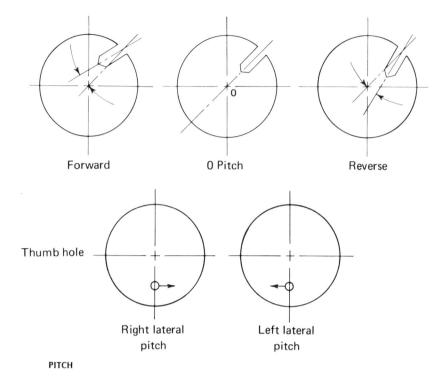

Forward   0 Pitch   Reverse

Thumb hole

Right lateral pitch   Left lateral pitch

PITCH

Left lateral (side) pitch is a drilling away from the palm of the hand, while *right lateral (side) pitch* is a drilling under or toward the palm of the hand. In left and right side pitches, the opposite is true for left-handed bowlers.

Another way of relating forward, reverse, left and right lateral pitch is to designate the pitch in reference to the emblem of the bowling ball. Drilling toward the emblem is forward pitch; drilling away from the emblem is reverse pitch; and left and right lateral pitch is simply drilling to the left or right of the emblem. Left or right lateral pitch can be used with forward and reverse pitch.

The *web* or *bridge* of a bowling ball is the distance between the finger holes, usually one quarter to three eighths of an inch. The *bevel* is the rounding of the thumb and finger holes after the holes have been drilled.

Bowling balls are constructed with what is termed a weight block. This is the area of the ball that will be drilled. It is the heaviest part of the blank ball. After a ball is drilled, the allowable tolerances are three ounces difference between the top and bottom of the ball and not more than one ounce difference between the sides to the right and left of the finger holes

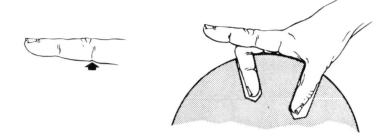

CONVENTIONAL SPANS—SPAN EXTENDS FROM THE BASE
OF THE THUMB TO THE SECOND JOINT OF EACH FINGER.

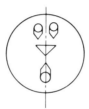

CONVENTIONAL PITCHES—DETERMINED BY CLOSE EXAMINATION
OF BOWLER'S HAND AND STYLE.

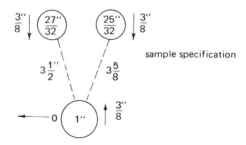

sample specification

CONVENTIONAL GRIP

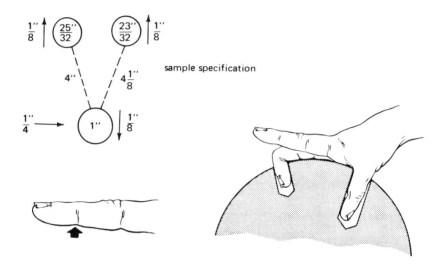

RELAXED FINGERTIP GRIP

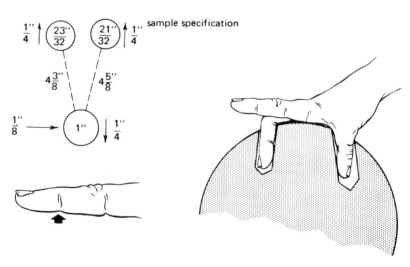

STRETCH FINGERTIP GRIP

or between the sides in front and back of the finger holes. Pros use these factors to their advantage, as will be explained shortly.

A conventional grip alignment has the center line splitting the center of the thumb hole and the middle of the bridge between finger holes. The conventional span extends from the base of the thumb to the second joint of each finger.

For years the recommended pitches were three-eighths inch forward for fingers and thumb with no side pitch. Now the ball fitter and the bowler should check the structure of the hand, fingers and thumb for stiffness or flexibility and adjust the span and the pitches accordingly for the most comfortable fit.

The semifingertip is usually drilled in a conventional alignment, but with a longer span. The span extends from the base of the thumb to a point between the first and second joint of each finger. Pitches are important and are utilized to ensure that the bowler does not hold the ball too long or lose it too early. Forward pitch gives a better hold and locks you in while reverse pitch allows easier release. Side pitches must be matched to the individual's physical makeup and bowling style.

The full fingertip is also usually drilled in a conventional alignment, but with a still longer span than either the conventional or semifingertip. The span extends from the base of the thumb to the first joint of each finger. In most cases the longer the span the less the pitch. And, in fact, reverse pitch is often needed to allow better release of the ball.

Most pros use the semi or full fingertip because it's easier on their hands and gives them an effective working ball. Casual bowlers find the conventional grip easier to handle as they have more of their finger in the ball.

With slight variations of span and pitches combined with the three basic grips, an unlimited variety of grips are easily obtained.

Johnny Petraglia, the Brooklyn lefty, who won more than $85,000 in 1971, most by a pro in a single year of tournament play, attributed part of his success to a thing he calls negative weight.

"My ball was hooking too much for me so I experimented with negative weight. It's obtained by drilling a ball so that the weight distribution will retard the ball's driving action until the last possible fraction of a second.

"A general rule is that top weight, finger weight and right side weight will produce more hook. I call that positive weight. Bottom weight, thumb weight and left side weight are negative weight—forces holding back the action of the ball.

"Any single weight factor can produce changes, and the combination of factors—positive, negative, thumb, fingers, top, bottom and sides—is practically endless.

"This is why it is so important that the man who drills a bowling ball

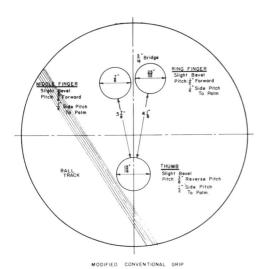

MODIFIED CONVENTIONAL GRIP

This grip provides comfort and more lift because of weight shift to fingers due to added pitch. My thumb goes into the ball only half way past the first joint

Bill Lillard.

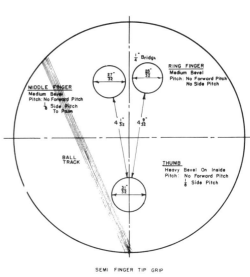

SEMI FINGER TIP GRIP

This grip feels very comfortable to me since pressure on the ball is evenly distributed.

Tom Hennessey

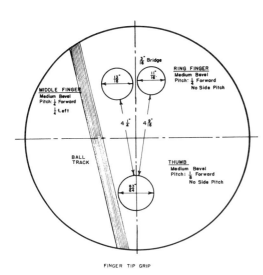

FINGER TIP GRIP

With these span measurements and pitches, I am able to get a sufficient amount of lift and consistency of release while using very little exertion in carrying the ball during backswing and delivery.

Jim Spalding

MODIFIED OFFSET SEMI-FINGER TIP GRIP

I use this type of grip to get more lift and roll on the ball. I use Nagy grips.

Buzz Fazio

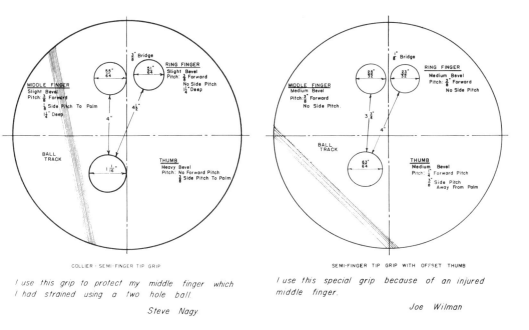

COLLIER - SEMI-FINGER TIP GRIP

I use this grip to protect my middle finger which I had strained using a two hole ball.

Steve Nagy

SEMI-FINGER TIP GRIP WITH OFFSET THUMB

I use this special grip because of an injured middle finger.

Joe Wilman

know what it is all about. It's vital for him to know the exact weight of the ball he is drilling, how much he will remove, and the different actions the various drillings could cause."

A bowling ball is a sturdy piece of merchandise, but the life of a bowling ball in the hands of a pro is usually a short one. The pros utilize weight and balance and carry a number of differently drilled balls to use on the varying lane conditions they come up against.

Longtime star Bob Strampe once remarked, "If the pros could carry them, they'd probably have one ball for each lane they roll on." The late great Steve Nagy changed bowling balls almost as often as he changed socks. Asked what he did with his old bowling balls, the Hall of Famer scratched his head, "I really don't know. I don't keep one long enough for it to get old."

Teata Semiz, the rugged New Jersey pro, has been the recent champ, using more than fifty bowling balls a year. He gives the usual reasons, different balls for different conditions, but also admits, "There is no doubt that a new ball gives me a mental lift, a new outlook on the game. The mental side is just as important as the physical, and that goes for any bowler of any average. Any time you feel that it will help is a good time to get a new ball."

If there's a secret in bowling balls it's learning how to use them properly. No grip will do miracles for your game. Any proper grip, fitted to the bowler in a manner that will help him cast the type of ball most satisfactory to him, will improve his game and give him the best of the odds.

If a bowler doesn't know what's best for him, and most don't, then let a pro do the job of analyzing, fitting and drilling.

BOWLING PINS

There are three types of bowling pins—standard wood, plastic coating a wood core, and all synthetic (nonwood).

For all practical purposes the all-wood pin is no longer in use, and no fully synthetic pin has been able to make the grade, so the pins in use are the wood core with plastic coating.

A regulation pin is 15 inches high, give or take 1/32 of an inch. At its widest point it cannot exceed 4.797 inches. The weight of pins varies greatly, as pins as light as 3 pounds 2 ounces and as heavy as 3 pounds 10 ounces are acceptable, provided they do not vary more than 4 ounces in each set. Pins in each set must be uniform in appearance, including construction, material, finish, labels and neck markings.

Pins may be constructed with one solid piece or with two or more laminated pieces of wood and must meet a host of ABC specifications in regard to balance, moisture content, finish, design, measurements and maintenance.

However, even within these strict confines pins can very greatly. A perfectly matched set of pins will fall better than a set using the 4-ounce tolerance. Different manufacturers apply the plastic differently and treat the wood differently.

Bowling center owners buy different pins for different reasons. Some want the pin that will last the longest, regardless of how well it scores. Some want a good scoring pin, regardless of how long it lasts. Most want a fair combination of both.

If pins are extra heavy the bowler must play a tighter pocket and come in higher on the headpin because of the increased deflection of the ball. If the pins are light a good hook ball seems to go right through them. Other pins bounce around rather easily and aid bowlers as they bounce from the kickback to the alley bed.

Pinfall is an important factor and a bowler must learn to adjust his angle of pocket entry according to the action of the pins. The ball is called upon to knock down over 33 pounds of wood and plastic. It needs all the help it can get.

ABC BOWLING PIN MEASUREMENT SPECIFICATIONS

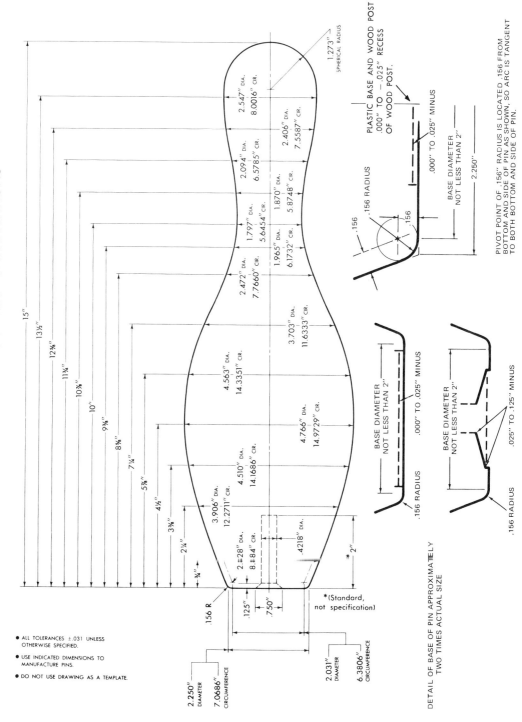

- ALL TOLERANCES ±.031 UNLESS OTHERWISE SPECIFIED.
- USE INDICATED DIMENSIONS TO MANUFACTURE PINS.
- DO NOT USE DRAWING AS A TEMPLATE.

15"
13½"
12¾"
11¾"
10⅞"
10"
9⅜"
8⅞"
7¼"
5⅝"
4½"
3⅜"
2¼"
¾"

1.273" SPHERICAL RADIUS

2.547" DIA.
8.0016" CIR.

2.406" DIA.
7.5587" CIR.

2.094" DIA.
6.5785" CIR.

1.870" DIA.
5.8748" CIR.

1.797" DIA.
5.6454" CIR.

1.965" DIA.
6.1732" CIR.

2.472" DIA.
7.7660" CIR.

3.703" DIA.
11.6333" CIR.

4.563" DIA.
14.3351" CIR.

4.766" DIA.
14.9729" CIR.

4.510" DIA.
14.1686" CIR.

3.906" DIA.
12.2711" CIR.

2.828" DIA.
8.884" CIR.

.4218" DIA.

.156 R

.125"
.750"

*2"

*(Standard, not specification)

2.250" DIAMETER
7.0686" CIRCUMFERENCE

2.031" DIAMETER
6.3806" CIRCUMFERENCE

DETAIL OF BASE OF PIN APPROXIMATELY TWO TIMES ACTUAL SIZE

BASE DIAMETER NOT LESS THAN 2"
.000" TO .025" MINUS
.156 RADIUS

BASE DIAMETER NOT LESS THAN 2"
.025" TO .125" MINUS
.156 RADIUS

PLASTIC BASE AND WOOD POST .000" TO –.025" RECESS OF WOOD POST.

.156 RADIUS
.156
.156

.000" TO .025" MINUS
BASE DIAMETER NOT LESS THAN 2"
2.250"

PIVOT POINT OF .156" RADIUS IS LOCATED .156 FROM BOTTOM AND SIDE OF PIN AS SHOWN, SO ARC IS TANGENT TO BOTH BOTTOM AND SIDE OF PIN.

The better bowler usually prefers pins that don't fall too easily, thus putting more accent on the skills of proper angle and proper action.

CLOTHING

Would you believe that old-time bowlers rolled important matches wearing high-collar shirts and ties?

Today casual comfort is the byword, for two reasons. One, because you look more like a bowler, and two, clothing should in no way restrict a bowler. You can't bend properly if your waist and legs are restricted in any way. The armswing is vital in bowling and it must be free to achieve the pendulum effect. This is impossible with a tight shirt or blouse.

The outer garments should be as loose-fitting as possible while still maintaining style. Take a look at any TV show featuring pro bowlers and you can see that bowlers can hold their own with any athletes when it comes to sharpness of dress, and still not lose any of their athletic prowess.

Don't neglect clothing that can't be seen. Socks are very important. Too thin and you may find your feet bruised and callused after a stint on the lanes because your shoes become loose and rub through the socks. Too thick and you might feel cramped in and also end up with a blister.

Underwear is an individual preference. Some like undershirts to absorb the perspiration. Some like none at all because they like to perspire freely. Shorts can help give extra abdominal and back support. In the female's case, women's lib with respect to the no-bra look should be discarded when it comes to bowling. Foundation garmets help keep all parts of the body firm. With all the movements bowling takes, any unnecessary flapping should be avoided, purely in the interest of higher scoring, of course.

The various stretch materials on the market are perfect for bowling apparel.

SHOES

Proper footwork is essential in bowling. Just as the ball should fit properly, so should your bowling shoes. The left foot, for a right-handed bowler, is the slide foot. Therefore, the left bowling shoe is designed to aid that slide. Normally the left sole is leather, though other materials can be and have been used. The right foot is the braking foot, so the sole is usually made of rubber or a substance that will aid in the braking effort.

The opposite is true for left-handed bowlers or right-handed bowlers who finish on the wrong foot.

Shoes range in price from a few dollar bills to a few ten-dollar bills. They range in style from loafers to some that would pass for proper evening wear. Practically all bowling shoes these days are low, though high-top shoes, the norm in the early days of bowling, can be custom made for those who feel they want more ankle support.

Support is the key word when it comes to bowling shoes. They must give you a firm anchor. They must be comfortable and give in the right places, yet still give you the support you need. A bowler spends many hours in his bowling shoes. If they bother him or hurt him in any way, he won't care much about his game, and the shoes will see to it that his game is likely to be a poor one.

BAG

Once you have a ball and shoes you need something to carry them in, and again, bowling bags offer a world of colors, materials and prices.

A bowling bag should have enough room for the ball and shoes to fit without crowding, also room for a towel and other bowling accessories you might want to carry.

Most pros have two-ball bowling bags. One of the chief assets of a two-ball bowling bag is that with all the extras the pros carry around, they have room enough for one ball.

If you intend to do plenty of tournament bowling which necessitates traveling, sacrifice style and material for a rugged bag that will hold up under the rigors of baggage handlers.

6

THE LANE
AND THE LANE TRACK

A regulation bowling lane is constructed of wood. It is 62 feet $10\frac{3}{16}$ inches from the foul line to the pit, and the distance from the foul line to the center of the headpin spot is an even 60 feet.

A lane is between 41 and 42 inches wide, and the lane plus the gutters measures between 60 and $60\frac{1}{4}$ inches.

When a bowling lane is constructed, it's done board by board. One board after another is piled up and put together with special nails along every 15 inches of its length. Each board is about as close as you can get to one inch so that a lane is made up of approximately 42 boards. That's the maximum. Some lanes have as few as 39 boards. This is very important to the bowler, particularly the pro bowler, as will be discussed many times.

The lane is made of maple and pine. Maple up front for about 15 feet, then pine, then more maple for about the last half dozen feet of the lane to the pit. The maple is harder and stronger and that's why it's used where the lane gets the most pounding, up front and down where the pins are. The pine, softer, holds down the middle where the ball should be rolling along at a smoother pace.

The important fact to remember is that a lane is made up of individual pieces of wood. Each has its own characteristics as to grain, hardness, ability to absorb moisture and wear and tear. Because each board is different, it will react differently from the repeated friction it gets from the rolling or bouncing bowling ball.

Both maple and pine are sanded and resanded and conditioned with lacquers and oils. They are also buffed. The surface must be free of all continuous grooves and a maximum tolerance of a mere 40/1000 of an inch is all that is allowed. Some of the best furniture wouldn't pass that test.

It is only with a full understanding of what makes up a bowling lane that the scope of the problem of lane maintenance can be understood. That is clearly pointed out by one of the world's greatest experts in that field, Remo Picchietti, who wrote a book on bowling maintenance as a science.

Picchietti discusses such things as crowning (the raising of the center of a lane because of expansion of boards), feathering (damage to the edge of boards caused by hard finishes) and the familiar high board (a much misused term describing a lane's condition). Atmospheric conditions may cause a board or more to contract or expand a bit. If a ball rolls over this area, its course is changed. Most boards contract and leave a low spot, yet the term *high board* is used to identify the condition.

As Sam Baca, the Professional Bowlers Association lane expert, points out: "The professional lane man is almost obsolete. In general he has been replaced by an automatic or semiautomatic lane maintenance machine. If the machines are not maintained properly they can create poor dressing patterns and drastically affect the lane conditions."

Every sport boasts that it is the sport of inches. Bowling really is a sport of inches and nowhere is it more important than on those one-inch boards. The average bowler is not expected to know too much of the detail of lanes and lane conditioning. But if a bowling ball does strange things on the lane, a bowler should be able to detect when he is at fault and when the lane condition has something to do with it.

With the pro it's vital that he know enough about lanes and lane conditioning. It's his living.

The lane starts at the foul line. The foul line, the border that determines a legal or illegal delivery, can't be less than three eighths or more than an inch in width. It must be clearly and distinctly marked on or embedded in the lane. It actually extends from the lane to and onto any walls or posts adjoining or within reach of the bowler.

Behind the foul line is the approach, often called the runway. It must be clear and level and not less than 15 feet in length. Many are longer. Depressions or grooves in the approach are limited to one-fourth inch. It is usually constructed of hard rock-maple wood.

The most comfortable and most logical starting point for a right-handed bowler is between the 10th and 15th boards from the right, which lines

ABC REGULATION BOWLING LANE DIMENSIONS

SECTIONAL VIEW

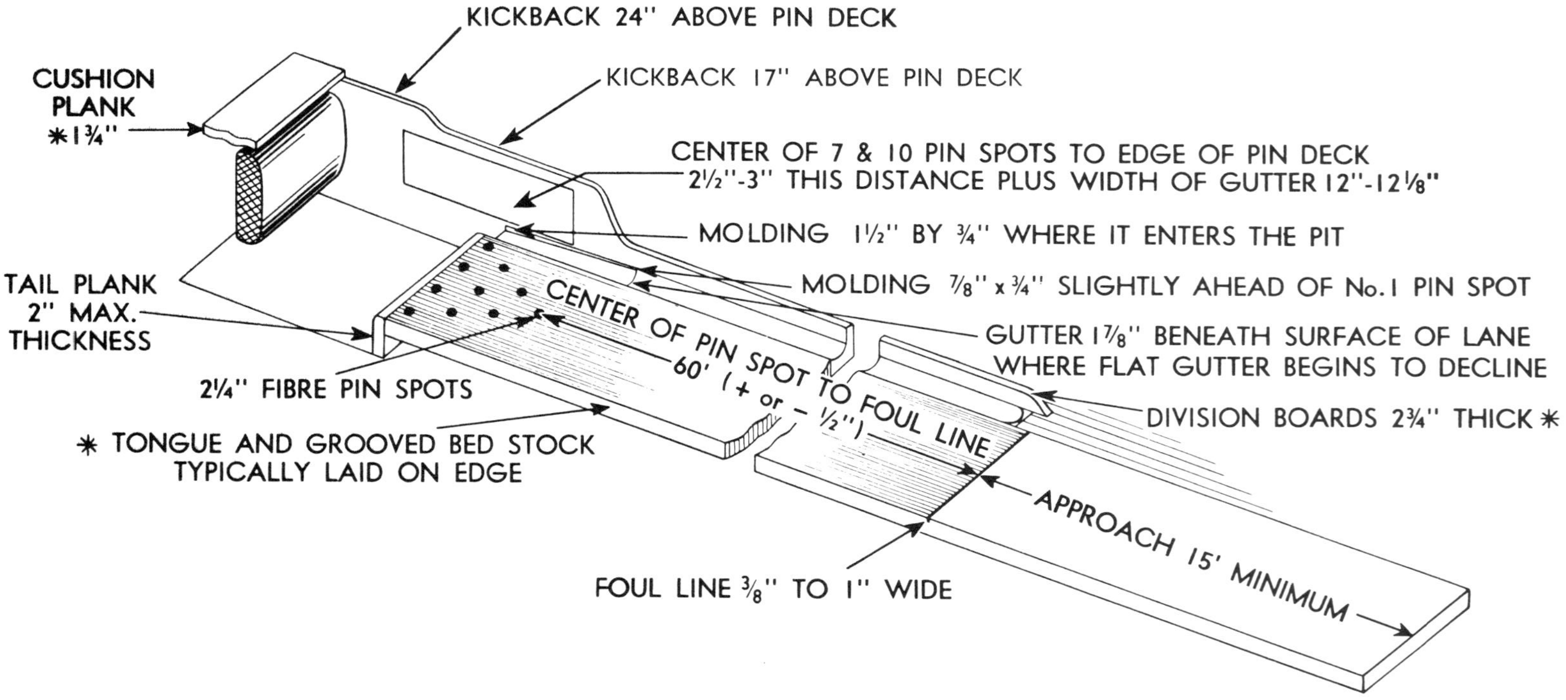

KICKBACK 24" ABOVE PIN DECK

KICKBACK 17" ABOVE PIN DECK

CENTER OF 7 & 10 PIN SPOTS TO EDGE OF PIN DECK
2½"-3" THIS DISTANCE PLUS WIDTH OF GUTTER 12"-12⅛"

MOLDING 1½" BY ¾" WHERE IT ENTERS THE PIT

MOLDING ⅞" x ¾" SLIGHTLY AHEAD OF No. 1 PIN SPOT

GUTTER 1⅛" BENEATH SURFACE OF LANE
WHERE FLAT GUTTER BEGINS TO DECLINE

DIVISION BOARDS 2¾" THICK *

APPROACH 15' MINIMUM

CENTER OF PIN SPOT TO FOUL LINE
60' (+ or - ½")

FOUL LINE ⅜" TO 1" WIDE

2¼" FIBRE PIN SPOTS

TONGUE AND GROOVED BED STOCK
TYPICALLY LAID ON EDGE

CUSHION
PLANK
* 1¾"

TAIL PLANK
2" MAX.
THICKNESS

* TONGUE AND GROOVED BED STOCK
TYPICALLY LAID ON EDGE

up between the second and third arrows. Give or take a few boards, this is known as the track. The constant rolling of the ball in the same general area results in the lane finish and the lane becoming worn, even though it is minute. It's hardly enough to measure or detect in most cases, but the tiny, almost invisible depression is there, and it is another highly important area of bowling.

You can find the track easily enough. Look for the darkened area between the second and third arrows, roughly the 10th to 15th boards. Based on the amount of play, this area could be shorter or wider.

In general the ball will hook most in the track. Inside or outside the track it will hold or straighten out. When you discover where and just how the track on the lane on which you're rolling works, you're well on your way to playing the lane properly.

Dick Weber firmly advises average bowlers to use the track. "The track is where the ball reacts the most. So adjust your game around it. Roll your ball in the track, to the left or right of it. There's only one main track on each lane and it could vary greatly from lane to lane and bowling center to bowling center. It is a great guide. A professional wants his own best track. And he uses the lane track to blaze his own particular track."

With the increased bowling in this country and the advancing age of many bowling centers, the track, in many instances, becomes more pronounced. This can cause problems. A ball may look perfect going into the pocket, then jump (hook sharply) at the last second, or it may be going merrily toward the pocket and stop hooking.

The track can be a big advantage. It can also contribute much to causing fits. When bowlers talk about not being able to find a line, they aren't talking about going fishing. They might mean that if they roll the ball in the track it hooks too much, and if they roll it out of the track, it won't come back over the track.

Lanes must be resurfaced when they fail to meet American Bowling Congress requirements: a levelness within a tolerance of 40/1000 of an inch, and freedom from any depression, groove or high spot or cross tilt exceeding that same tolerance. Resurfacing simply means the removal of all coating material by a sanding operation so that the surface is once again as flat as possible, at worst within the ABC tolerance limits.

A newly resurfaced lane is about as flat as it's ever going to be and there is no track. That means that on a newly resurfaced lane the ball will do only what the bowler does to the ball. There will be little or no lane help in regard to a track. Pro bowlers usually prefer a condition such as this, even though the average bowler might not.

It is economically impossible for a proprietor to resurface his lane too many times. The cost is high for each job, but probably more important is the fact that each resurfacing takes some of the wood away. Too frequent resurfacing and the lane would be sanded away too soon. The bowling proprietor's income and livelihood are predicated on a certain life expectancy of a bowling lane.

Lane conditions have changed over the years because the lane finishes and lane maintenance have changed. In the early days the owner of a bowling center was usually a bowler, and he personally took care of his small center, right down to doing the lanes.

Today's bowling center is huge and machines have taken over the job of caring for the lanes for the most part. In general, lanes hook more because they are used more. They "break down" easier, a term used by the pros which simply means that conditions change. A lane that wouldn't hook very much on the early squad of a tournament turns into a racetrack (excessive hooker) by evening.

The pro bowler is aware of the changing conditions. No longer does he have to work hard to develop a hook. Almost any bowler can roll a hook these days.

Arguments rage as to what is and what isn't a proper lane condition. Naturally a bowler prefers a condition on which he scores his best. A pro bowler learns to accept conditions the way he finds them, and to do his best whether he likes them or not. The pro learns to adjust to all possible conditions he might encounter.

7

CUSTOMS AND COURTESY

Few bowlers realize the enormous investment necessary to build a bowling center and to keep it in operation. A single bowling pin may cost as much as five dollars or more. But that really is only pin money.

If you add up the cost of land, building, machines, furniture, snack bar, lounge, meeting rooms, nurseries and all the other equipment needed to keep a single lane going the way it should, you're talking in the neighborhood of $35,000. You can almost buy a home for what it costs for a single lane. And if more bowlers took this fact into consideration, they might treat a bowling center as a home away from home.

Smokers should dispose of their cigarette and cigar butts in the proper receptacles for two reasons: one, so that the expensive rug stays plush as long as possible, and, two, because a cigarette or cigar butt on the lane could cause problems of sticking or sliding. The same goes for all food or drink. If you must eat or drink while bowling, keep both food and liquid away from the playing area.

Kicking the rack won't help you and it won't help the rack either. The same goes for all other equipment in a bowling center. Most of it is expensive. Much of it is delicate. When your temper or carelessness causes you to interfere with, disrupt or destroy any of the equipment, you are hurting everyone's enjoyment of the game, including your own.

When you or a teammate or any other bowler is tempted to take out his problems on the equipment, just ask the simple question, "How many bowlers would kick the rack if the rack could kick back?"

Courtesy on the lanes during actual competition is just the accumulation

of common sense over the years, rules of bowling etiquette that have evolved to benefit all bowlers.

When two bowlers are ready to go, the man on the right has the right of way. This is only in those instances where there is some doubt and indecision could cause a traffic problem. If a bowler on the left is ready to go while the bowler on the right is stepping up, then the bowler on the left goes right ahead.

In a pro tournament this deference is extended to a pair of lanes on each side. Reasons for this are numerous. The pros are putting on a show and this gives spectators a chance to see each bowler better. The pros are rolling for big money. Bowling is their living and this extension gives them a clear field of concentration. They don't waste time. They know what they are going to do and once they set themselves, they go; so despite this clearance on both sides, they really don't take much more time than their amateur counterparts.

In the same vein, stay on your own lane. Jumping and leaping are fine, but when one's body english extends to the adjoining lane it can throw the other bowler off at the least, and at worst could cause a serious collision.

Don't needle an opponent or even talk to him as he is preparing for and going through his shot. Bench jockeying strictly on the bench is okay to a point, but if you give it, be prepared to take it too.

Don't use someone else's equipment (ball, bag, shoes, accessories) without permission. In sanctioned tournaments each five-man bowling team must have at least three bowling balls. In the doubles and singles each individual must have a ball.

Take all the time you need to get set on the approach, but don't waste any time getting on the approach when it's your turn to bowl. You're there to bowl. Keep wandering to a minimum. Be seated when you're not bowling. It's a good time to study the lanes and think out what you want to do on your next shot.

Try to be a good winner as well as a good loser.

You call a bowling ball a bowling ball until the day you drop one on your foot or catch your fingers between two of them. If you are careful on the ball rack and in the ball return area, you won't be tempted to call it anything else.

8

LET'S START

On the lane approach dots are set into the wood, usually at the 12- and 15-foot mark. These are the distances most suited to most bowlers, and they are there so you can have a proper guide for foot placement at your starting position, better known as stance.

Remember, these are your initial guides. To find exactly where to stand, with your back to the pins place your heel about two inches in front (on the approach side) of the foul line. Now take the number of steps in your approach, whether it's one or eleven, and add a half step for good measure. Turn around and you've got your approximate starting distance from the foul line.

Check it closely in relation to the row of dots. If you're an inch behind one of the marks, remember, and use the same distance all the time. This starting point could vary as much as a couple of feet for different bowlers. People of the same height have different-sized arms and legs. And even people with the same measurements have different strides, swings and slides.

Another important point is to know where to stand from side to side. The center dot, or slightly right of center, should bring your approach to the line so that the ball will roll over the second arrow, generally accepted as a good starting point. Make sure your shoulders are square, parallel to the foul line.

There's an additional series of dots two inches before the foul line and other markings on the lane itself, such as the previously mentioned arrow; more details about utilizing them later.

9

STANCE

Stance, which combines posture, manner of standing, position of feet and hands and arms, is an important fundamental stage.

There is no such thing as a true stance. The old book on stance has been rewritten. Ray Bluth peeks over the top of his ball. Other pros hold it chin high, shoulder high, waist high or down as low as arms will allow.

For years it was considered standard to hold the ball in midbody position. Many pros now hold the ball off to the right, to more easily achieve the desired straight arm swing.

Hall of Famer Therm Gibson, a husky 230-pounder, showed that the bowler on the heavy side could compete with the best. The late Gibson will always be remembered for the $75,000 he won in a few minutes on the PBA's "Jackpot Bowling" TV show, a record amount of money for so short a time. He held his ball far off to the right.

Both feet should be close together, soles firmly on the floor. It's often helpful to place the left foot slightly ahead of the right.

In general the higher the ball is held, the more speed a bowler will generate without extra effort. So if you're a bowler with too much speed, try the ball a little lower in your stance. If you would like a little extra speed without really thinking about it, then hold the ball a bit higher. The height of the ball should be the position most comfortable for you.

For the three- and five-step delivery, the weight is on the right foot; for the four- and six-step, the weight is on the left foot. The elbow should be tucked into the side. The wrist should be straight and fingers must be placed firmly into the ball to get the proper feel at the start.

Most pros are fairly upright in body position, but nobody will get up-tight should you prefer a slight crouch or even a stoop. Some bowlers find that slightly bending their knees helps them. The key in the stance is to find the best position for yourself, physically and mentally, to plan your shot. There is no wrong and no right. But once you find what you feel is your best stance, stick to it so it becomes a part of you, making only minor adjustments from time to time or lane to lane. The more a bowler does without thinking too much about it, the better off he is.

A TIP FROM GUS LAMPO

"You hear so much about keeping your shoulders square to the line that you might be deceived. Sure you should be square, you must be square, but to your target, not always to the line. Often when lanes are hooking out of the building you must face away from the line. And when they're real tight, you had better angle your shoulders toward the pocket or the ball will never make it."

A TIP FROM ALLIE CLARKE

"Your body seldom has the balance it should have prior to the start of your approach. So even when you're set and ready to go because you think you're perfect, try counting up to three. The little hesitation brought on by the counting does away with two things, too much tenseness and too much relaxation. It puts your mind on the count, and by the time you go on three, your body is about as ready as it's ever going to be."

A TIP FROM RAY BLUTH

"Always be sure you have the needed separation between standing position and target. If your target is the third arrow, you shouldn't be standing on the third arrow. You should be standing so that your approach will bring your ball over that third arrow. This will vary with every bowler."

Bluth has always been famous for his little black book. Actually, it sometimes isn't black, and sometimes it isn't a book, but merely a sheet of paper.

Bluth has always been a meticulous person and this carries over into his bowling. He charts every lane he rolls on throughout the country. He records the best place to stand, the best target for him, whether the lane hooked or didn't hook, and any other characteristic of the individual lane, as he sees it.

Even if he never rolls on the same lane again, over the years he has a file on almost every conceivable type condition and what it calls for in the way of adjustment. If a bowler can chart where he's been, it may help him where he's going.

CORRECTION CLINIC—STANCE

If your weight is not distributed properly the first step may lag too much and prevent any speed at all during the approach. Make sure that most of the weight of the body is on the nonstarting foot.

A ball held too high and dropped abruptly can easily cause a bowler to run well ahead of his backswing. A bowler must take special care to find the proper position of the ball with respect to distance from the floor. There is no set rule as it depends on the varying physical attributes of each individual bowler. The height the ball is held has a direct effect on the distance of the pushaway, length of first step, height of backswing and position of upper body at completion of approach.

A ball held too low often leads to rushing and imbalance.

Once a bowler has determined where he wants to hold the ball from side to side he must be on the alert to see that his ball goes into the backswing close to his knee and in as straight a vertical line as possible from the start of the pushaway to the top of the backswing.

If the elbow is not close to the body, even touching the hip, the bowler is apt to release the ball with an outside-in swing, also known as a roundhouse swing.

The thumb should not drop below the nine o'clock position in the stance or a bowler may top the ball. A topped ball spins ineffectively in an unpredictable manner.

A bowler should have the "feel" of the ball. A helpful procedure here is to flex the fingers to loosen them up and also move them in and out of the holes until you establish a firm but relaxed grip.

10

PUSHAWAY

You have been advised on how and where to stand before you start. Now you must start. Your first moving action is the pushaway. In the three-step delivery the pushaway and first step are one and the same for all practical purposes. In the four- and five-step there is for many a slight hesitation, the steps beginning without too much direct action on the pushaway. For others, it is easier to push the ball prior to the first step and let the feet catch up to the ball movement.

The pushaway is just what it says, getting the ball away from your body, and it is of vital importance because it's the start of your timing of ball with feet. A bad start could mean a bad finish unless there is some sort of corrective action during the rest of the approach. This is the reason some bowlers have hitches, speedups or slowdowns in portions of their approach, to compensate for earlier mistakes in coordination.

Push the ball from the body gently, forward and slightly down. The left hand supports the weight of the ball, and the fingers and thumb of the right hand are inserted all the way. Extend your arms without any undue stretching. Take care not to allow the ball to drop straight down. You are attempting to achieve as smooth a movement in as near a perfect pendulum motion as possible.

Lifting the ball is an enemy here, too, as it may keep the ball before you too long and hurts your footwork. Dropping the ball too abruptly gives the wrong arc and jerks the shoulder from its desired square position.

If your knee is directly above your toe and your shoulder above your knee, you know your body is aligned properly up and down.

PUSH AWAY

BALANCE LINE

STRAIGHT ARM PENDULUM

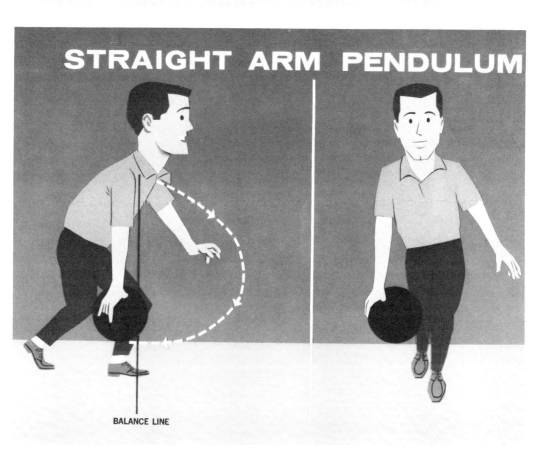

BALANCE LINE

A TIP FROM LOU FRANTZ

"Rushing is a problem with most bowlers, but taking too much time is just as bad. You can tie yourself into a knot when you get on the approach. First thing you know, you're so tight and tense you can't bowl. Make up your mind as to what you're going to do while you're on the bench, not when you're on the approach."

CORRECTION CLINIC—PUSHAWAY

If the pushaway causes any strain or takes any extra effort and the first step doesn't feel natural, it's simply that the pushaway is too long. A shortened, more natural motion will correct it.

If the ball is pushed too high, an uneven swing, jerky motion and dipped shoulder will result. A lower height, causing a natural arc as the ball starts down, is what you should seek.

The ball weight should initially rest on the nonbowling hand. If it is switched to the bowling hand too soon, the swing is likely to be erratic. Keep the nonbowling hand under and to the center of the ball.

11

BACKSWING

It's difficult enough to know what's going on in front of you when you bowl, much less what's going on behind you.

The backswing, therefore, should be the natural result of your stance and your pushaway. Never force a backswing. You are looking for an even arc. You want what is natural for you, though the backswing should never be higher than the shoulder. It should also be close to the body.

The more you bend and lean forward, the higher your backswing will be. The more erect you are, the shorter it will be comparatively. An exaggerated pushaway will force the swing back with too much force and throw the hip and body off. Wrist should be firm. Just picture your arm as the swinging pendulum of a grandfather clock. The slightest push from any angle will knock the pendulum from its smooth path as it rocks back and forth. Don't do anything that would rock your arm during this phase of delivery.

BACKSWING

BALANCE LINE

TIMING

BALANCE LINE

A TIP FROM DICK RITGER

"Get free, stay free, keep free. The pendulum swing you hear so much about is simply a free swing of the arm from the shoulder, with no help. If you don't have a solid, steady, dependable swing you will probably muscle the ball in tense situations.

"When you muscle the ball you don't swing free. You carry the ball. You help the ball and you force the ball. You give the ball help it doesn't need if you have the proper pendulum swing. And in this case, helping hurts."

A TIP FROM BILLY HARDWICK

"I find a short backswing works best for me, and I keep it pretty consistent. The only real disadvantage to a short swing is that you can't generate too much speed. You can adjust speed with your fingers to some degree. I can roll the ball faster and still keep a good roll by spreading my first (index) and my last (pinky) as far apart as is possible and comfortable. This gives me more of my hand on the ball, and a faster ball. If I need less skid and more roll, I place the fingers as close as possible, and with the short spread I just can't get any extra speed."

A TIP FROM FRED LENING

"When you're wide in body build, you must fight not to move your bowling arm away from your body. You naturally tend to cross your mark by coming around. Get that elbow in even if in the process your elbow brushes your side. Then at least you know you're as close as you can get.

"Bowlers with heavy body builds don't have the leverage in their arm swings that the thinner bowlers do, so that's why it's even more important for them to avoid that old bugaboo, rushing the foul line."

12

DELIVERY, APPROACH AND FOOTWORK

Since pros themselves use almost every conceivable type of delivery, they do not condemn any particular delivery, providing the bowler using it has been around long enough to master it. The ultimate answer to what type of approach to use is in performance.

THREE-STEP DELIVERY

The three-step delivery is a quickie. The left foot starts out and the ball is pushed away at the same time, all during that first step. The ball moves back quickly and well into the backswing on the second step. On the third step the left foot is at the foul line and in solid position for delivery of the ball while the ball is still coming forward. Now the arm must do most of the work to bring the ball forward without much benefit from the rest of the body to help the swing.

That's the main reason the three-step delivery is frowned upon by most experts. It takes more strength than the four- or five-step. It is tiring over the longer grinds. It is too fast. And while only three steps are taken, most bowlers using this delivery will take steps that are extra long.

STARTING POINT. Place both heels at the foul line, take 4½ brisk walking steps from the foul line and turn around. This is your correct starting position.

STANCE

STANCE. Left foot forward, right foot back. Stand erect, knees slightly bent. Support the weight of the ball in both hands. Place your fingers and thumb into the proper holes and hold the ball to the right side.

FIRST STEP

FIRST STEP, the pushaway, is the first and most important step. As you move your right foot forward, push the ball forward and down in one easy motion.

SECOND STEP

SECOND STEP. Once in an arc motion, the ball starts into the backswing. Keep your arm close to your body. Move your left foot forward. Your left arm swings away to a natural balancing position.

THIRD STEP

THIRD STEP. The ball reaches the top of the backswing, not above shoulder level. The right foot is forward, shoulders parallel to the foul line. Lean forward and down.

FOURTH STEP

FOURTH STEP. As your left foot slides, your right arm comes forward in one simultaneous motion. Perfect timing is achieved when your sliding foot and right hand reach the foul line together. Left knee is bent, shoulders are at right angles to direction of delivery, your right arm comes through to lift the ball over the foul line.

FOLLOW THROUGH

FOLLOW THROUGH. Upon releasing the ball your arm should follow through over your right shoulder. Hold this position, balanced on your left foot until the ball hits the pins. If you cannot maintain this balanced position, your delivery has not been smooth and easy.

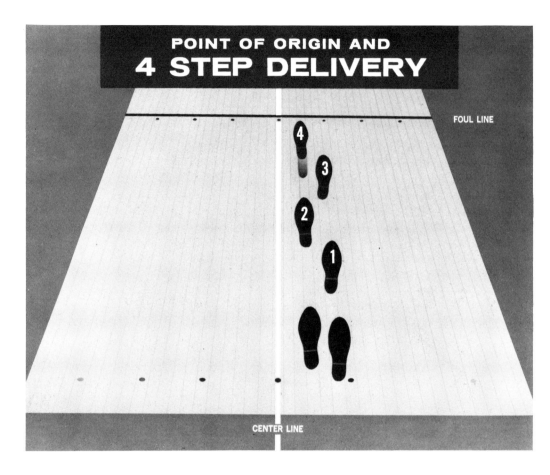

POINT OF ORIGIN AND
4 STEP DELIVERY

FOUL LINE

4
3
2
1

CENTER LINE

FOUR-STEP DELIVERY

The first step of the four-step delivery is the right foot moving into a natural step, at the same time pushing the ball away from the body. Don't leap or lunge, but don't pussyfoot either. Stay away from giant steps or baby steps, but if you must lean in one direction, go to the shorter steps.

On the first step, the left hand is still bearing most of the weight of the ball. Remember not to push the ball up. Its own weight should send it down properly.

On the second step, the ball is at your side and moving into the lower portion of the backswing as your left foot touches the floor. Your arm should be close to your body. The left arm starts seeking a natural balancing position without any help from you.

The ball reaches the peak of the backswing toward the end of your third step. Momentum is speeded up, the arm is still straight, swinging freely from the shoulder. The first two steps and the movement of the body should supply the necessary speedup. At the end of the step the ball should be at its peak of the backswing, but never higher than the shoulder, and the shoulder should be parallel to the foul lines.

The downward motion starts easily and the knees bend more, lowering the body to prepare the left foot for the fourth and final step, which is generally a long slide reaching completion an inch or two before the foul line. So long as a bowler is consistent, this distance may vary a few inches with no problem.

In the fourth step the knee is bent and the bowler slides on his left foot, using his heel as a brake at the moment of release. The ball and the left foot should be at the foul line together, and the body bends forward at this point. The left foot should be firm. The right foot should still be in contact with the floor and used as a balancer or brake. However, some star bowlers manage to balance themselves with the right foot in the air.

A good method to determine the effectiveness of your approach is your ability to hold your final position at the foul line until after the ball has made contact with the pins. If you can't, though it may not necessarily hurt your scoring ability, it does show that your delivery can be smoother.

FIVE-STEP AND OTHER DELIVERIES

There is a great difference between the three- and four-step deliveries. There is little difference between the four- and five-step deliveries. The five-step, basically, is a four-step with a preliminary step prior to putting the ball into motion, though some experts do manage to incorporate the pushaway into the first two steps of a five-step delivery.

There are good reasons for a five-step delivery. If for any reason a bowler wishes to start on the left foot, then the five-step is the answer. It will also help if a bowler's steps are too long. A five-stepper must necessarily shorten his steps or he will go over the foul line. Bowlers who prefer a faster type approach rather than a leisurely one find the five-step better for them.

CORRECTION CLINIC—DELIVERY

Don't carry the ball too long. If the nonbowling hand, used to hold most of the weight, is not released soon enough, it throws the body balance off.

Keep the nonbowling hand on the ball as long as necessary to help with the weight of the ball as it starts the backswing, no longer. This would be near the bent right knee in the second step of the four-step delivery. It is also at this point that the nonbowling arm moves off naturally to aid the body balance in the rest of the approach and delivery.

Don't force the ball down at the start of the backswing. It could cause you to drop or push the ball at delivery time.

If the ball is too high in the backswing, the hips and shoulders move around. In most cases the problem is caused by a too long pushaway or a body position too low. When the pushaway is too long, the bowler will probably pull the ball through the arc. Here what you need is to shorten the pushaway and to check to make sure the body is straight.

If the body is ahead of the ball on the final step, check to make sure that the ball and the sliding foot are in unison.

When a bowler's hand is finishing across and in front of his body he is obviously pulling the ball. The points to check here are the thumb position, because there is a possibility the thumb is coming out too soon, and the wrist and the elbow to make sure the wrist is as straight as possible and the elbow is close to the body.

Dropping the ball is a common problem. First check your grip. Your thumb should be fully inserted into the thumb hole; a hanging thumb gives only a limited grip and is one of the leading causes of ball dropping. Have your fit checked carefully. There is no reason for a bowler not to put his thumb in all the way. A bowler should always take a firm, not tight grip on the ball. The feel of the grip should be in the fingers and thumb only with no undue pressure on any other muscles. If this isn't so, have your fit checked.

If your approach is obviously rough or not suited to you, then it's time to start from scratch, beginning with a slow speed and moving up faster and faster until the approach matches the normal walking or running style of the bowler. Usually the slower the better, but if your personality is geared to a faster pace, then you must find the right pace for you.

Some bowlers do better with a heel-toe type step or a shuffle, rather than another type of step. Both are worth a try.

13

BALL RELEASE

The ball is released at the end of the final step as the left foot completes the slide. The ball should be rolled well over the foul line without lofting or hurling it too far down the lane.

One of the most important factors at the point of ball release is a deep knee bend of the left leg. Bending the knee helps raise the heel from the floor, which makes sliding easier and prevents an abrupt stop at the line. If the knee is straight, the leg is straight, and you will be forced to stop too quickly and release the ball with a jerky motion.

How far over the foul line should you roll the ball? This varies from a few inches to a foot among the top pros. A simple test is to place a towel along the foul line. If you don't clear the towel you're not getting the ball over the foul line. Always remember that your arm should be reaching out toward your target and that the ball is released on the upswing, and you will automatically get the ball out on the lane.

If the ball is released behind you, at your side or anywhere on the bowler's side of the foul line, the release most likely will be ineffective. Release at these points makes it practically impossible to impart the lift needed for action on the ball, and it also cuts down on accuracy.

The ball release is the objective for everything you do from the time you pick up the ball, through your stance and delivery. Think about it, know what you're doing.

Again, it should be a natural result of a smooth delivery and a pendulum

RELEASING THE BALL

RELEASE

BALANCE LINE

armswing. Much emphasis is properly placed on making sure the thumb comes out first, and bowlers should remind themselves time and time again to let the thumb come out of the ball first.

Don't worry about it. Too much undue concentration and worry about the thumb release will have the opposite effect. Most bowlers don't have to worry. If the ball fits properly and if the bowler goes through his approach properly, there is no way the thumb won't come out first. The downswing of the ball will naturally allow the thumb to release first.

Every bowler has heard of the handshake and "V" finish positions. These are the positions formed by the thumb and the forefinger when the ball is being released for a hook. It is roughly the ten o'clock position.

Once the thumb is out of the ball, the ball rests on the fingers. You can't hear enough times that this is when the action of the ball is imparted by the lift of the fingers.

A TIP FROM LOU SCALIA

"Every bowler is told about the handshake, how the position of the hand in bowling should be the same as the position of the hand when you reach out to shake hands.

"What most bowlers are never told is when the hand should be in that position. So they try it from start to finish and end up at the point of ball release attempting to release both thumb and fingers at the same time, which is obviously wrong.

"The handshake should come only when you're through with your delivery, after you have gone through the ball. Into and at the completion of the follow-through is when you should have the handshake look."

CORRECTION CLINIC—PROPER FIT

Once a bowler has learned to release the type of ball he desires, whether the ball is straight or any variety of hook, he doesn't need any special grip. Once the bowler understands his own style of release, his bowling ball should be fitted to him in a manner to help him cast the type of ball most satisfactory to him.

A ball should be fitted, keeping in mind the double motion of a bowling ball, that of revolving while skidding, and that revolutions are imparted to the ball by the fingers after the thumb has been released.

Since it is imperative that the fingers leave the ball last, it becomes equally imperative that the finger holes in the ball be fitted and drilled to a size that enables the bowler to hold on with his fingers after the thumb has been released. The longer the fingers remain in the ball on delivery after the thumb has been released, the better opportunity the bowler has to impart revolutions to the ball with the fingers.

This result can be enhanced with the size of the holes and with the various pitches and can be achieved regardless of the type of grip the bowler prefers.

Many of the most common faults are directly related to a poorly fitted bowling ball. The fit is often the culprit when a bowler is attempting to correct faults in any phase of his game.

For instance, a ball that is too heavy can cause the shoulder to drop, a forced, jerky hurried approach and swing, a turned wrist and a dropped ball.

If the ball is too light the result could be too high a backswing, too much speed, too much deflection causing weak hitting power, and a ball that hooks too much.

A too wide span leads to strain on the hand and wrist and a late thumb release, while a too narrow span causes too much hard gripping, loss of control, a dropped ball, and a weak hook or none at all.

When the thumb is too large there is a tendency to knuckle or crimp the thumb which strains the hand and wrist. It hurts a free swing and is a cause of dropping the ball on the backswing or at the release.

If the thumb is too small the release is almost impossible, the thumb will come out too late and the result is often a lofted ball, a skidding ball, or one that has little power.

If the fingers are too large you will drop the ball at release, and if they are too small you will overreach at release.

The wrong pitches in a ball will cause similar problems. The fit of the ball, meaning the size of the holes and the pitches, must be designed to allow free, natural release and at the same time aid the bowler as much as possible in the type ball he rolls.

14

FOLLOW-THROUGH

Probably no single phase of the technique of bowling has been more mis-interpreted, more overstressed and less understood than the follow-through. It is too often considered both the cause and the cure-all of bowling ills. If the ball backs up, doesn't hook properly, drops from the hand, leaves splits or does anything else to cause a problem, follow-through becomes the battle cry of correction.

Actually the follow-through is the continuation of the hand and arm in the direction in which the fingers lift the ball at the point of release. Without some definite lift of the fingers as the ball is released, follow-through has little meaning. It will not correct the error of dropping the ball behind the foul line. It will not remedy a faulty release.

The greater the lift of the fingers, the more decisive the action of the ball. If the ball is released with the fingers behind the ball, the follow-through is a continuation of the forward effort used in lifting the fingers correctly.

When the fingers pick up from the outside, or the right side of the ball, the follow-through is normally straight up if a limited hook is desired.

The greater the lift of the fingers across the ball, from right to left, the greater the follow-through the hand and arm will take across the body. The greatest number of revolutions are imparted to the ball when the lift, almost a pull, of the fingers and the follow-through of the hand and arm are across the center of the body and the hand and arm wrap around the waist. This would be the extreme and used only under certain lane conditions.

FOLLOW THROUGH

BALANCE LINE

CORRECT

INCORRECT

Where you let your arm go—whether straight through, up to the left shoulder, across the body or even off to the right—is not important. Just make sure you don't choke or cut short the follow-through in any manner.

Follow-through only has meaning when the lift of the fingers requires that the arm continues its motion in accentuating the action of the ball.

CORRECTION CLINIC—FOLLOW-THROUGH

In his eagerness to score well, a bowler will be intent on steering or guiding the ball to the pocket. The action used in such attempts results in the hand stopping short during the follow-through. Another possible reason for the cutting of the follow-through is a premature bending of the elbow. Make sure the entire motion of the follow-through is a one-piece action.

15

THE TYPE OF BALL
YOU ROLL

Your thumb acts as a lever to hold the ball on the fingers. This permits an easy release of the thumb prior to the release of the fingers. However, that thumb is the quarterback when it comes to calling the type of ball you will roll. The position of the thumb and fingers at point of ball release, and the amount of lift imparted by the flats of the fingers when the ball is resting on them momentarily after the release of the thumb, are the key to the action the ball will take.

Using a clockface as a guide is the best way to determine what a ball will do and how to get it to do what you want it to do.

If the thumb is at twelve o'clock and the fingers are directly behind the thumb, the ball will revolve forward and go straight. Actually, since few bowlers can be perfect in ball release, a straight ball is more theoretical than anything else. However, for bowling purposes, the twelve o'clock thumb position will give you a straight ball.

The secret to making a bowling ball hook lies in making sure that the thumb is to the left. Using our clock again, you would find that the thumb at eleven o'clock will produce a limited hook, ten o'clock a little more hook. If you wanted the maximum roller type hook, nine o'clock is the spot for the thumb.

The thumb position is only a part of rolling an effective hook ball. When the thumb, in its proper left-of-twelve-o'clock position, is released,

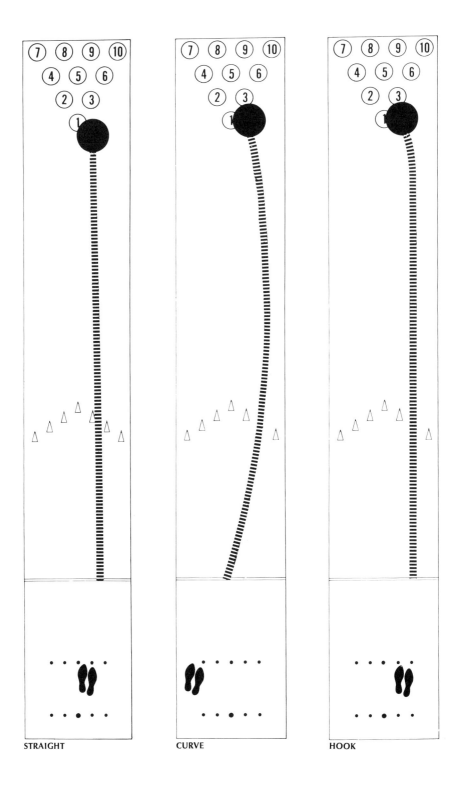

STRAIGHT CURVE HOOK

the ball falls ever so slightly to the left; here the finger lift, often called pickup, takes over and keeps the ball revolving in the direction it has already started to take.

The curve ball is nothing more than a large or maximum hook ball. It must be rolled with slow speed and exaggerated lift. If it isn't, it's just a fast hook ball.

Since the position of the thumb to the left of twelve o'clock and the lift of the fingers impart counterclockwise revolutions to the ball and cause it to hook, the reverse is true when the thumb is right of twelve o'clock and the revolutions imparted by the fingers are clockwise. You then have a reverse hook, better known as a backup.

The backup is ineffective unless it is rolled from the left side of the lane by a right-hander, thus making it like a left-handed hook. The straight ball is only slightly more effective, and its great claim to fame is that it is easier to control. But it is just as easy to control a slight hook, and the ball is much more effective. The curve ball is difficult to roll with any consistency, and more difficult to control.

So of the four types of ball, you can quickly discard the backup, the straight ball and the curve. That leaves the hook, and it is the best for all bowlers.

Every bowler, just remembering and concentrating on the simple thumb position (to the left of twelve o'clock) and the finger lift (you can gain this feel by inserting your fingers into a bowling ball and rolling it across the floor without the aid of the thumb in the ball), can roll the hook ball in varying degrees. Size of the hook is not important. It's more important to develop a simple, comfortable hand position.

CORRECTION CLINIC—YOUR HOOK

If you're getting too much hook it could be that you are releasing the ball too early, rolling it too slowly, or have an angle that is too extreme. In addition, closely check your thumb position and move it closer to twelve o'clock. As a last resort reduce the amount of lift applied with the fingers. If the ball is not hooking, the same tips in reverse—more toward pocket angle, thumb position closer to the nine o'clock position or additional finger lift—will help. There is only one area where things should remain constant, in ball release. This should be smooth all the time, and no attempt at coming out of the ball earlier or later should be attempted. Worry about the thumb release only if it is causing a problem. Otherwise keep it constant.

16

BOWLING BALL TRACK

The ball track or roll of the ball is easy to find on any bowling ball. This is where the ball rolls down the lane. As it rolls it picks up minute particles of lane dressing, dust and oil, and also some tiny nicks caused by the friction of the ball on the lane. Together they form a band on the ball.

If this track, band or line is between the thumb and finger holes, you roll what is known as a full roller. It rolls over the full circumference of the ball and is a good mixing ball, though it doesn't hook much. The bowler who rolls a full roller uses practically no wrist in his ball release.

The semiroller or semispinner produces a track outside the thumb hole an inch or so. It's sometimes called a three-quarter roller because that's about how much of the ball's surface makes contact with the lane. The semiroller produces a good hook and the release to obtain it combines lift and slight wrist action.

The spinner is just that. Its track is way down, covers only a small part of the circumference of the ball, and the ball spins down the lane much like a top. It doesn't have much mix. The spinner is a result of plenty of wrist twist at the point of ball release.

In addition to telling you what kind of roll your ball takes, the ball track also tells you how consistently you roll the ball. The narrower the band, the more consistent you are. If you vary, the track or band will vary too and become wider.

There have been champions with each type of roll. However, the spinner is the least effective, and these days bowlers who can roll any of the three types resort to the spinner only when they want a ball to hold or set in the pocket. The semiroller is the most popular and the ball roll used by most of the top pros in the country.

If you are scoring well with any of the three types of roll, stick with it. If you're going badly, it may be worth it to switch, but only if you're rolling the spinner or full roller and want to go to the more effective semi-roller.

17

TARGETING

SPOT BOWLING

In bowling you're shooting at a target, the 1-3 pocket, some 60 feet away. It's reasonable to assume that if you can hit a target much closer and still knock the pins down, then you've come up with the shortcut of all time.

Basically, that's the theory of spot bowling, used in one form or another by the majority of the world's greats in bowling. Once you have reached the stage where you can roll the ball approximately the same way each time, you are ready for spot bowling.

The following are very important: You must start in the same position and finish in the same position. You must maintain the same speed. You must hold the same angle. Any variation of any part of your approach, delivery and ball release will affect you when you're a spot bowler.

Many bowlers, told they should become spot bowlers, pick their spot on the lane, hit their spot five times of six, and discover that they have left everything but the kitchen sink. Hitting the spot from three different angles will result in three different hits. The same is true of speed of the ball.

But assuming you do have the basic fundamentals in tow, where do you spot?

Glenn Allison spots right at the foul line. "I had trouble getting to the line when I was a youngster. I felt if I spotted too far out on the lane I'd get my feet tangled up, so I developed my style of selecting a spot at the line."

Most pro bowlers use a spot about 15 feet from the foul line, based on the arrows embedded in the lane at five-board intervals. Years ago there were no such targets and a bowler had a select a board, distinguished by a darker or lighter color from the surrounding boards.

Some strong, sharp-eyed bowlers such as Barry Asher select spots as tiny as the crack between two boards. Asher is one star who advocates spotting way down the lane, 30 to 40 feet from the foul line. "Hit your spot way down and the ball will be more consistent," says Barry. "It isn't that much more difficult to hit your spot, it helps you reach, and when you hit your spot, the ball is really solid.

The spot you pick and the distance you choose are an individual thing. Whether you select a dot, an arrow, a light or dark-colored board or the crack between boards, at inches or many feet, the theory is the same. It's easier to hit a spot closer to you, but when you miss the close spot, the error is larger at the other end. If your spot is way down, a slight miscalculation will have less effect.

Once you find your spot, watch carefully after you release the ball. See if your ball goes over the spot, and if it misses, count the number of boards it misses right or left. Then you can adjust. One of the advantages of spot bowling is that it gives you a guide. If you roll the ball over your spot perfectly and the ball doesn't do what it is supposed to, it's a clue that your delivery could be off the beam in some way. Or it could tell you about the characteristics of the lane, whether the lane is hooking or not, and where it is hooking most.

Once your ball goes past your spot area and you've made a mental note of how well you hit or how badly you missed the spot, you can raise your eyes to the pins to see the results. A true spot bowler sees the pins only when they are originally set, and the moment when the ball is going into the pins. The rest of the time the spot on the lane takes all his attention.

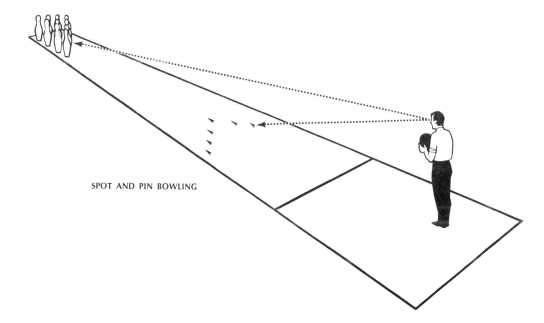

SPOT AND PIN BOWLING

PIN BOWLING

Pin bowling seems to be the most logical way to bowl. The pins are there and you want to knock them down. So you set yourself in a position you feel will take you to the foul line to release the ball in a way that will bring the ball into the 1-3 pocket, which is your target. You are basically drawing an imaginary line from where you start to where you want the ball to wind up, and you glue your eyes to your final target.

Most beginning bowlers find it easier to pin bowl. Once into the game they can move into spot bowling. Strictly pin bowling has one big disadvantage. You take too much time to discover why you missed the headpin or why you crossed over. These faults are more easily and quickly discovered by the spot and line bowlers.

LINE BOWLING

Line bowling, in any of its many variations, is probably the most widely used method of targeting. It is often called a combination of spot and pin bowling but refinement would probably be a better word. The line bowler checks his starting spot on the approach, the position of his left foot at the foul line at the finish of the approach, his spot on the lane and the strike pocket. But he uses two spots along the way, usually the arrows and the area of the splice.

The two spots are by no means universal and there's a wide variety of preference. The main point is that the two spots make for more checkpoints along the way.

In using the line system, don't try to look at two spots at the same time. That may seem funny but many bowlers try to do it. A little practice and you'll learn how to shift your gaze from spot to spot along with the ball as it goes along the imaginary line.

A TIP FROM MIKE McGRATH

"Pick your spot and do your best to hit the spot you select but don't worry if you don't hit it perfectly. You can still roll well so long as the ball hits in a certain area, and so long as you don't try to aim or force the ball.

"If you're playing a lane inside (more toward the center or to the left of center) make sure you are always on your mark or inside your mark.

"If you are playing outside (more toward the gutter) make sure you hit your mark or go outside it. That simple formula gives you an area rather than a single spot, and it will help convert some bad shots into good shots."

A TIP FROM RALPH ENGAN

Optical illusions or just bad eyesight can cause bowlers to hit the wrong spot or mark even though they're hitting what they consider the proper target.

"One bowler told me he had no trouble in hitting his spot and proved it by rolling 11 of 13 balls over the 13th board. Only one problem. He thought he was rolling his ball over and hitting a spot on the 10th board.

"That meant that the bowler was actually three boards to the left of his proper target. If he watched another bowler in practice and saw the bowler going over the 10th board and scoring, he would then try to hit the 10th board. And when he thought he was hitting the 10th he was actually hitting the 13th.

"The problem can be solved by taking six dimes and placing one on each of the boards from 8 to 13. Then aim for the second arrow or 10th board. Keep aiming for the 10th board. It will soon become evident what board you hit when you aim for the 10th. Simply check the dimes you move. It could be the 10th, but more than likely it will be two or three boards to the left or right of the 10th.

"With the results of this simple test, all errors of eyesight or any possible optical illusions are erased. If you must hit the 10th board to score and you must aim your ball a couple of boards to the left or right of the 10th to hit it, you must make this adjustment accordingly. Many bowlers do this correcting with instinct, and don't realize it. If there is a possible problem in this area, the simple dime test will show a bowler where he really is hitting, not where he thinks he is hitting."

18

READING A LANE

There is no great mystery about any bowling lane. It will either hook more, hook less or act normally, and by normally is meant what is normal for you.

Always start out in your own natural way, rolling the ball the way you prefer. If your normal ball goes into the nose or crosses over, you know you have a hooking condition. If you're light or miss the headpin the lanes aren't hooking.

Sounds almost too simple, doesn't it? The difficult part is coming to a decision. You can't judge the lane condition until you're sure you are rolling your ball properly. This takes a couple of balls to be sure. Then if you start fiddling around with adjustments it may be the fifth or sixth frame before you really feel sure.

In many cases that's too long. For the pros, who move after every game, it could be disastrous. There are shortcuts in reading lanes. If possible watch the bowlers preceding you on the lanes, and if you know them well enough, ask them, just to get a general idea. Look at the lanes closely. If there's oil, you can bet they'll be on the tight side and not hooking too much. The same is true if you're the first one on the lanes that day or night.

If the lanes have been going all day, you can almost be sure that they will be hooking more than usual. Check the track. Watch every ball rolled. If a lane is such that every bowler seems to have trouble hitting the headpin, don't wait for a special message, accept the obvious signs given you. Reading a lane is simple if you use the methods of a detective and tie all the clues together quickly.

Don't prejudge or expect a lane to act the way it always has or is supposed to act. Lanes change, definitely during a day of much use, sometimes even in a single game. Be prepared.

19

SPEED

Because speed and power often go together, it's no great surprise that the natural inclination is to roll a bowling ball too fast. Too much speed is unnecessary and usually harmful. There are exceptions, of course, and two of them are Pat Patterson and Dick Hoover.

"When I bowled on the same team with Don Carter, Ray Bluth, Tom Hennessey, Dick Weber and Bill Lillard, I got jealous because they carried the pins so much better than I did on what looked like the same kind of hits," says Patterson.

"The armswing determines how fast you roll the ball," adds Patterson, "and when you're tall and have a nice, easy swing, you sometimes have a lot of natural speed. But most bowlers don't have natural speed; they generate it themselves."

A ball normally skids, then rolls and turns. The lift imparted to the ball results in a certain number of revolutions. For best action of ball against pins, these revolutions should begin in the ball's final movement into the pins. Too much speed and the ball will skid too far. It will then go into a partial skid and the full revolutions of the ball will never be realized.

A speed ball will push the pins high into the air rather than keeping them down on the pin deck to mix and possibly knock some other pins down. Since the ball actually hits only four pins, the 1-3-5-9, it is absolutely essential that you get pin mix. Speed is an enemy of a good working, mixing ball.

Less action in the pin area means that on seemingly good pocket hits you will leave more of the corner pins. The more corner pins you leave, the greater chance you have of leaving pocket splits such as the 5-7 and 8-10.

For those who are natural speed bowlers like Patterson and Hoover, and can't cut down the speed without serious style problems, be aware of the speed problems.

Give the ball more angle into the pocket to make up for the extra skid. Play the high and tight pocket, well into the 1-3, because a speed bowler can't depend on light-hit strikes. On spare shots hit every pin with the ball, as speed causes chops, particularly on the double wood setups such as the 1-2-8 and 1-2-4-8 and the fences such as the 1-2-4 and 1-2-4-7.

The big advantage of speed is accuracy, so make the best of it.

An excessively slow ball is just as bad as the too speedy ball. Here the ball's action is spent early, and by the time it hits the pins it's like a top that is almost completely unwound. The rate of deflection is very high and the ball literally bounces away from the pins after contact.

Pro bowlers are fairly adept at changing speeds, but it is one of the most difficult of all bowling arts. Unless your ball is glaringly too fast or too slow, work with your normal speed, and adjust through other basics of the game such as stance, pushaway and approach.

20

A STRIKE

Careful study of photographs, movies and TV's instant replay reveal exactly what happens when a right-hander scores a perfect strike. The ball moves into the 1-3 pocket. The number 1 pin hits the 2 and in domino-falling fashion the 2 hits the 4 and the 4 takes out the 7. On the right side of the lane the 3 pushes into the 6 which fells the 10. The ball continues driving on its own path, taking care of the 5 and 9 pins. The 5 is pushed into the 8 and that's it.

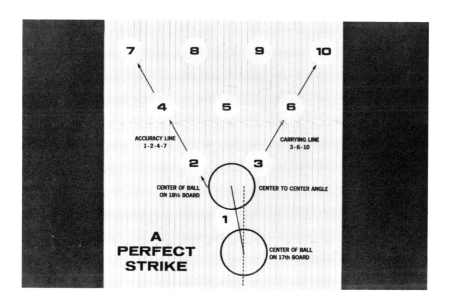

On a perfect strike, the ball itself hits only four pins. Pin action takes care of the rest.

The 10-pin tap, the heartbreaker to many bowlers because the 10 stands on what seems to be a perfect pocket hit, is normally the result of faulty pin action. When the ball strikes too much of the 3 pin, because of the wrong angle, a late sharp-breaking hook, a flat ball or any other reason, the 3 hits the 6 too full and the 6 goes too far to the right, and around the 10 pin without touching it.

Though it's difficult to explain to a bowler who has just suffered through a 7-, 8- and sometimes even a 9-pin tap on what looks like a perfect hit, a close look will show that a pin either went around or hit another pin and bounced up and over the pin it was supposed to take out.

However, if a bowler constantly leaves certain single pins on hits that look excellent, then it can't be attributed to bad pin action, but to the angle the bowler is using, the type of ball he is rolling, or the action he is putting on the ball.

21

SPARE SHOOTING

The only way not to miss spares is to get all strikes. But sometimes they are so scarce you'd gladly trade your best friend for one. In the meantime you're faced with spare leaves.

There are 1,023 different spare leaves, and on a bad night you might feel you left every single one.

Spare bowling is basically dependent on one thing, the proper angle. Always use as wide an angle as possible—but don't use more than the width of the lane. On certain lanes you can get some extra space to the left or right when you're shooting end pins. The problem comes when you get used to the extra space and then go to another bowling center in which a rack or some other part of the structure prevents you from using that extra space.

There are three spare angles, middle, left and right, sometimes called 5, 7 and 10, based on those pins. Spare bowling takes concentration, and you can use the same method of bowling as you do for strikes, spot, pin or line.

Two vital rules to remember in spare shooting involve angles. First, on all middle spares, use the strike angle. Second, for the pins standing on the left, move to the right, and for the pins standing on the right, move to the left.

In using these cross-lane angles it is vital that the bowler use a straight-line approach. However, now the shoulders should be parallel to the target, not to the foul line, as is constantly preached when shooting for a strike. It's the same thing: on a strike attempt you must be square to the strike target; on the spare you must be square to the spare target.

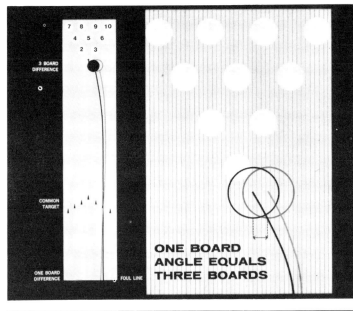

ONE BOARD
ANGLE EQUALS
THREE BOARDS

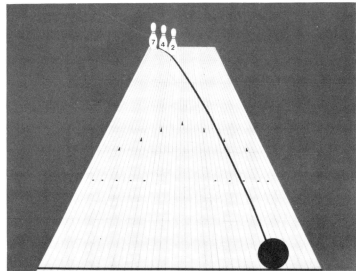

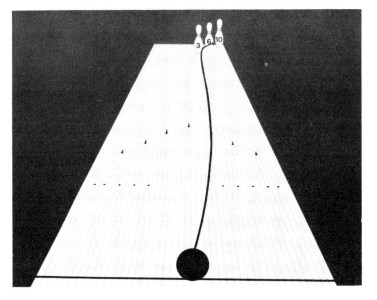

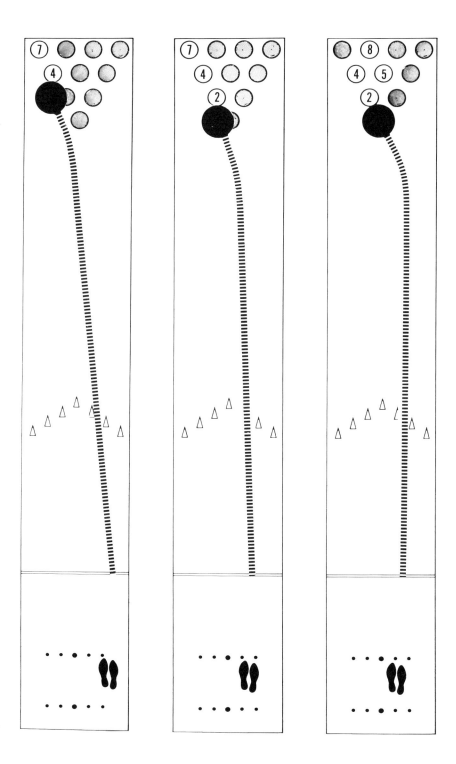

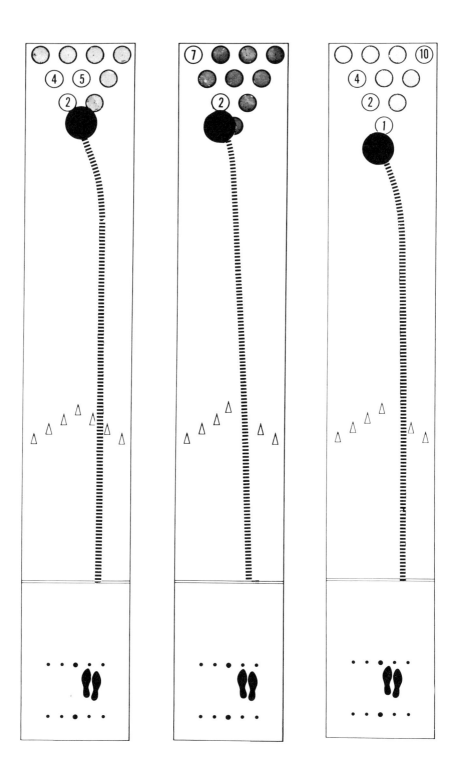

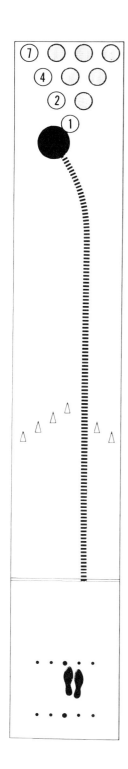
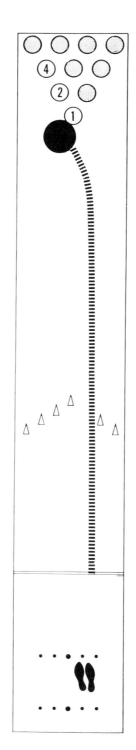
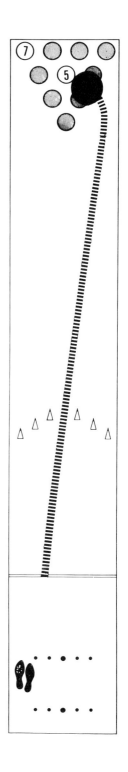

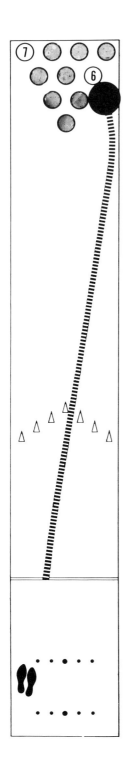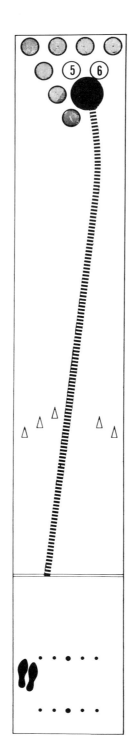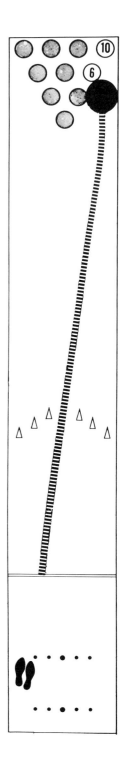

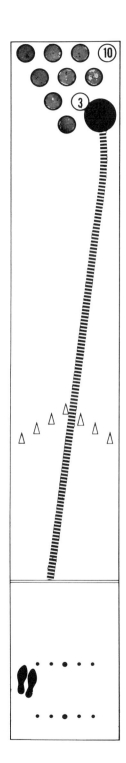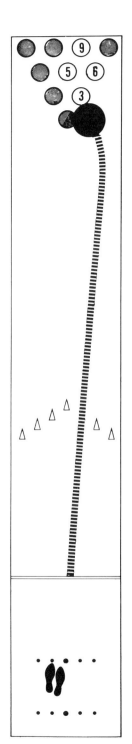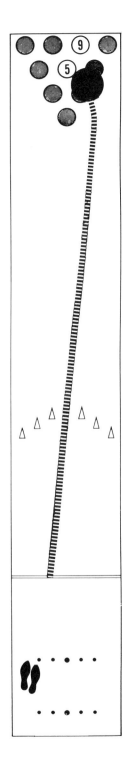

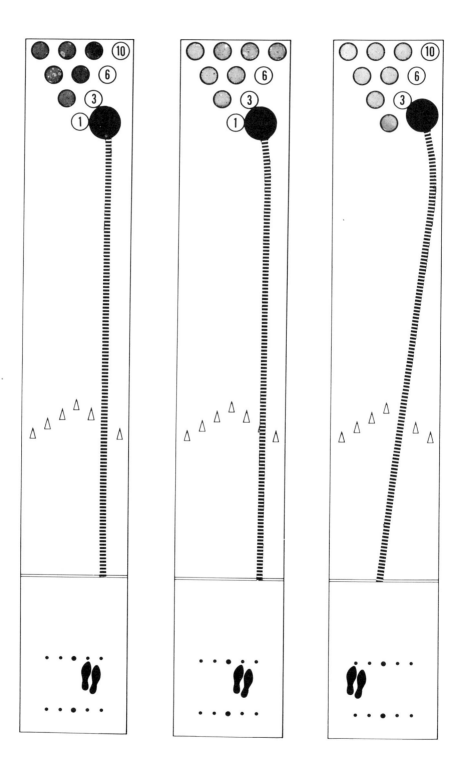

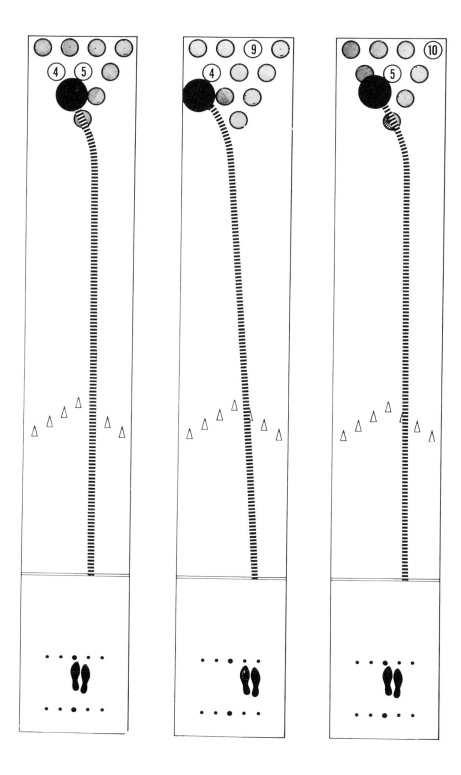

If it seems that pros are unconcerned about spares it's because they have trained themselves automatically to assume the proper angle and stance for the various spare shots while still taking into consideration the lane condition.

Pros more than anyone realize the full value of a spare. Each missed spare is approximately 11 pins. It could go as high as 15 pins. There are many games in which a pro just can't rack up the strikes. If he can hold his spares and toss in a double or a triple along the line, he can still top 200, despite the small strike total.

For the average bowler the spares are even more important. In any night's three-game session, if you're in the 150 to 170 average group, you miss anywhere from three to nine spares. If you can make one more spare a game than you do now, your average will increase ten points plus. Just one additional spare each night and your average will be upped three to four points.

Some simple basics in spare shooting include hitting all single pins as full as possible, making sure you cover every pin with the ball when possible, and learning a key pin in every setup so that when you're shooting for any spare, no matter how many pins, you can forget about all but the pin that is the key to making all of them fall.

The right side usually gives right-handed bowlers more trouble than the left. The following method has helped many bowlers. It's simple and it works.

Take a position to the left of the center of the lane and line up your right shoulder with the third arrow from the right and the 10 pin. Make sure you face toward the third arrow and the 10 pin. Keep shooting this approximate angle until you make the 10 pin without too much trouble. This now takes care of all spares where the 10 pin is the key.

If the 6 pin is the key pin, just move three boards to the right on the approach and do exactly what you did to zero in on the 10 pin. And if the 3 pin is the key, move six boards to the right of where your approach mark was for the 10 pin.

Correction ratios are very important in spare shooting. If you are close to where you want to hit, move only a board or two at a time. One board to the right on the approach normally means the ball will hit the target areas three boards toward the left.

Ratios must be generalized because excessive hooking or extremely tight (not hooking) lane conditions will change these ratios.

It must also be noted that though the cross angle is the best way to shoot spares, many of the pros will not use this angle when shooting for such spares as the 2-4-5 or 2-4-5-8, mainly because they chop such spares so often, and want to cut the angle. Similarly, if a lane condition prevents your rolling what you consider the proper angle, find new key pins and a new angle. This is rare, but a bowler should be able to adjust.

SPLITS

Splits cover a wide range. The small ones are less difficult than some spares; the big ones are almost impossible.

With baby splits and the more difficult fit splits, the key is to hit fully the pin that isn't there.

For instance on the 3–10, 2–7, 4–5 or 5–6, a shot that would perfectly take out the 6 pin, 4 pin, or 3 pin, respectively, would work most of the time. With an extremely sharp-breaking curve ball, bowlers have been known to go between the 3–10 and 2–7 without getting any pins.

Actually these splits are made by hitting both pins with the ball, having the ball deflect from the front pin to the back pin or, when they're parallel, fitting the ball perfectly between them.

The wider 5–7 and 5–10 splits can be made only by sliding the front pin across to hit the rear pin, and the still wider 4–10 or 6–7 takes an even more skillful shot because the angle at which you must hit the front pin is smaller and leaves less room for error.

When you reach the 4–6, 7–10, 7–9, 8–10 splits you are in the almost impossible range. Here the best thing to do is to settle for the wood. Make sure of the one pin you can convert. However, if the pin means nothing in a situation where the conversion of the split could mean a win, then go for broke, by attempting to bounce the pins.

In the 7–10 and 8–10 and similar splits where the pins are parallel they are practically impossible because the ball cannot hit one of the pins at an angle to slide it across. Sometimes the pin is slightly off spot from pin action and this gives you an outside chance.

In the 1971–72 season a total of 3,125 Big 4 (4–6–7–10) splits were converted and 2,831 of the pesky 7–10 splits made into the spares. That isn't too many considering that something like a billion games were rolled, but it does take away the impossible tag to make these split leaves "almost" impossible.

All of the same attention paid to spares should be given to splits. Don't let the emotional aggravation of a split cause you either to miss it or to throw valuable pins away by a don't care attitude. And try to figure why you got the split and how to avoid more in the following frames.

A TIP FROM BOB STRAMPE

"On the tour you learn to deviate a bit. You learn how to straighten the ball to a degree. Since it's tough enough to master a single delivery, I certainly don't advise rolling a hook ball for strikes and a straight ball for spares. When you are forced to work to straighten the ball out, it goes against what you have worked to achieve in the way of style.

"When you're shooting that troublesome number 10 pin, move to the left on the lane but not so far that you feel the angle is crowding you. Keep your hand in a fairly open position with the thumb at approximately 12 o'clock and point the thumb at the 10 pin. Release the ball as normally and as relaxed as you can. If you're a hook bowler there will still be a certain amount of turn, but not enough to change the shot.

"What's true about the 10 pin is also true of various spares where a straight ball makes for easier conversion. Use angle and a slight hand variation to cut the hook a bit, but all within your normal style.

"Don't try to throw hard at the 10 pin or any other spare. This isn't normal and is difficult to gauge, but the tendency is to jerk the ball when you attempt to speed up unnaturally at irregular intervals."

22

CHECKLIST OF FUNDAMENTALS

Every now and then a bowler should check himself for fundamentals, or better yet, do it as a doubles team with a bowling buddy who knows his game.

Look the bowling ball over. Is it time to try a different grip? Should you go to a lighter or heavier ball? What about weights in regard to balance, maybe your local pro will have some advice worth listening to?

Check out your stance, paying full attention to your feet, weight distribution, knees, height the ball is held, alignment of the ball, where the weight of the ball is distributed, position of elbow, position of wrist, and thumb position as checked against the face of a clock.

In the approach the number of steps and size and speed of steps are all important.

Take a look at your armswing. Is it straight, inside-out, outside-in? Do you crook your elbow or loop your arm around? Does your backswing go to shoulder level or above, or is it waist high or lower? At the line are you balanced with a good knee bend?

What about your ball release? Is your palm up, down, right or left? Is the wrist firm or does it sag or rotate to the left or right? Finger lift is all important. Is it smooth and almost effortless with the proper feel? Are you conscious of the outside fingers and their relative positions to the middle and ring fingers?

Is your follow-though doing the job? What kind of action do you have on your ball? How many boards is it hooking? Is the ball carrying when it hits the pocket, or is it weak, or maybe too strong at times? Are you making your spares? If not, what spares are giving you the most trouble, and what are you doing about it? How much are you practicing?

It's always good to analyze your game as often as possible. You will have strong points which need little or no work at all. You will have weak points that need constant attention. An informed bowler has to be a better bowler. He must know his own game, be able to tear it apart and put it back together again making the weak parts stronger.

Over and over again the top pros will emphasize the fact that the greatest secret in good bowling is no secret at all, just a matter of always going back to fundamentals. Check them as carefully as an airline pilot goes over his checklist prior to every flight. He's going up, and that's one way your scores can go up too.

23

KEEPING SCORE

At first glance a bowling scoresheet looks like a combination of chicken tracks, a ticktacktoe game with numbers and a complicated mess of horizontal boxes made even more complicated by small boxes inside the big boxes containing secret symbols.

A few more glances and the scoring of the game becomes simplified.

First, a game consists of ten frames. On the scoresheet that's one horizontal line divided into ten boxes. Many times two smaller boxes or squares will be imprinted in the upper right-hand corner of the larger box.

In each of the first nine frames you roll one or two balls. If you knock all ten pins down on the first ball, that's a strike, and that frame is complete. If you don't knock all the pins down with your first ball, you are allowed a second ball. Knock the remaining pins down with your second ball and you have a spare.

A strike is worth 10 pins *plus* the number of pins you knock down with your next two balls. So you can score a maximum of 30 pins in each frame. If you score a strike in the tenth and final frame you are allowed two additional balls. If you garner all strikes, nine in the first nine frames, and three in the final frame, you would have a perfect game of 300, a score of 30 for each of the ten frames.

A spare, all pins down with two balls, is worth 10 pins *plus* the number of pins you knock down with your next ball. So the most you can score in a frame in which you have a spare is 20, 10 for the spare and 10 more should you come up with a strike on the next ball.

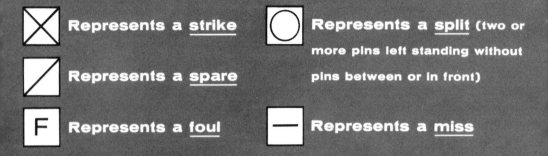

MARKINGS

$\boxtimes$ Represents a **strike**

$\square$ (with diagonal) Represents a **spare**

$\boxed{F}$ Represents a **foul**

$\bigcirc$ Represents a **split** (two or more pins left standing without pins between or in front)

$—$ Represents a **miss**

A Typical Scoresheet

1	2	3	4	5	6	7	8	9	10
⑦ −	✕	✕	8 −	✕	F 9	8 /	9 F	9 /	✕✕✕
7	35	53	61	80	89	108	117	137	167

If you fail to knock all 10 pins down with both balls, known as a miss or error, you simply record the number of pins.

For instance if you had a strike and then got 9 on two balls, you would have 19 in the first frame, 10 for the strike plus the total of the next two balls, then for the second frame you would show 28, the 19 in the first frame plus the 9 in the second.

The scoring markings are uniform the world over. A strike is designated by an ✕. A spare is recorded by using a /, although in some areas the line is reversed. A split is designated by a small circle (○) and the error or miss is recorded with a plain horizontal line (–). These last two markings are informational—they are not a part of scoring.

The two smaller boxes inside the large frame boxes are utilized to give a ball by ball count of the game, if you're interested in having a record. The first ball is recorded in the first of the small boxes. If it's a strike, nothing else is needed. If the bowler doesn't strike, the number of pins on the first ball is recorded in the box. If it's a split the circle goes around the number. In the second box goes either a spare or the number of pins felled on the second ball.

A split symbol is used simply to balm the bowler's ego. A split is a setup of pins remaining after the first ball has been legally delivered, provided the headpin is down and at least one pin is down between two or more pins which remain standing, for example, the 7–9 or 3–10, or at least one pin is down immediately ahead of two or more pins which remain standing, for example, the 5–6.

Since a split is much more difficult than a regular spare leave, the circle differentiates from the horizontal line, which signifies a miss.

The main thing to remember about scoring is that it is maintained progressively, frame by frame, and the actual score in one frame may not be determined until two frames later. This happens when a bowler racks up a string of strikes. A double (two strikes in a row) or a turkey (three strikes in a row) will happily delay the scoring.

Keep thinking in 10s, for a strike plus pins knocked down with next two balls, 10 for a spare plus what is knocked down with the next ball.

All bowlers, just as soon as possible, should learn how to project a score. No matter what frame the game is in a bowler should figure his and his opponent's potential. A match may seem hopelessly lost, but a little quick figuring will show that a triple strike against three open frames can pick up more than 50 pins.

Every center has scoring manuals to aid a bowler in this phase of the game. The best way to learn how to keep score is to keep score as often as possible until it becomes second nature.

Automatic scorers will no doubt be installed in all bowling centers of the future. Brunswick Corporation already has a highly successful scorer on the market and in use in many centers throughout the nation. AMF has a semiautomatic scorer, and other manufacturers are also in the field, or will be in the future.

However, automatic scoring or not, it's still a must to know how to score and how to analyze and project what could happen during a game, whether in team or individual play.

There are many rules in regard to scoring, most of them referring to legal and illegal pinfall and fouls. Such things as a dead ball, replacement of pins, bowling on the wrong lane, and unreasonable delay are all explained fully in the specifications and playing rules published by the American Bowling Congress each year.

One cardinal rule is that no pins may be conceded and only those actually knocked down may be counted. A standing pin, even if moved off its original spot, is never scored as a downed pin, unless it is standing in the gutter or anywhere else off the playing lane, when it is scored as down.

If there is some disagreement as to whether a ball was delivered legally or there was a foul or a question of legal pinfall arises, it is imperative that a provisional ball be rolled. Thus two different scores will be carried until the league, tournament director, local bowling association or American Bowling Congress makes the final decision on the matter.

24

SCORING AT
PRO TOURNAMENTS

Pro tournaments are long, a minimum of 42 games, at times even more. They consist of qualifying games in which a bowler is credited simply with the pins he knocks down and the match play finals in which a bowler is credited with the pins he knocks down plus an additional 30 pins for each game he wins.

To make it as simple as possible for spectators to follow the scoring standings, the PBA devised an over-and-under system. It's all there, easy to read, on the projected and magnified scoreboards above each lane.

A score of 200 per game is considered par for the pros. His entire score from start to finish is now determined by that all important 200 figure.

If a bowler rolls a 230 game, he has scored 30 pins "over par" and beside his name you will see a 30 written in black. If he shoots 170, he has gone 30 pins "under par" and a 30 will be inscribed in red.

From the first game to the last, the total is cumulative. If the figure is black the bowler is "over." If it's red, he is "under." The highest black figure is the leader, the highest red figure is the lowest in the field. At a glance a spectator can spot the leaders and the laggers.

If a spectator wishes to figure the bowler's average, it is easily done by taking the figure in black and dividing it by the number of games rolled, also noted on the scoreboard. For instance a bowler 120 pins over for five games is averaging 224. If the players are into the bonus system, the bonus pins must be subtracted before figuring the actual average.

The pro system has been adopted by many tournaments, and "over" and "under" have become a part of the language of bowling.

25

ABOUT BOWLING AIDS

John Powell, Jr., one of Ohio's all-time great bowlers, a bowling proprietor and a genius at merchandising bowling products, once said, "I usually will sell a dozen of anything that advertises it can help a bowler, no matter how good or bad the product may be."

How good are the almost endless array of products? It's no secret that pro bowlers are offered special cash incentives if they use certain bowling equipment and accessories, particularly on television.

However, no pro will endorse or use a product unless he believes it really will help his game and the game of other bowlers who use it. If the pros use them, you can be sure that they will not be a detriment to that particular pro's game. No pro will endanger his livelihood by a quick cashing in on a product that may hurt him in the long run.

So don't be afraid to try any of the bowling aids on the market. However, be cautious. Try them in practice first.

There are virtually hundreds of items. Most popular and most useful are the various types of finger and thumb inserts, gloves and wrist bands, and products to keep the bowling hand dry.

Bowling accessories are an important part of a game and a peek into any pro bowler's bag will reveal at least half a dozen different aids.

If you have a problem that can be helped with an aid, don't hesitate. But always be leery of the way-out gimmicks that promise you too much. Bowling aids are just that, aids. They are designed to help a bowler, not make a bowler.

A TIP FROM DON CARTER

"Many times when I'm applying a protective coating to my thumb or fingers before I bowl, a reporter won't really believe me when I tell him nothing is wrong. In bowling there must be a certain amount of friction between your hand and the ball. I patch the areas where I have the most friction, where it's possible to develop a sore spot or a blister.

"Know where your problems could arise. Once you're bowling it's difficult to treat a sore spot and still maintain your normal style. Like all other sports, you're more prone to injury in bowling when you're under-trained or overtired.

"If possible always try to roll a practice game or two prior to league or tournament play. But learn how to pace yourself, don't roll that extra game if you feel tired. And remember, three games in competition takes more out of you physically and mentally than twice that many in practice.

"If you are recovering from serious illness or an operation, take your doctor's advice. Don't try to come back too soon, but when you get the green light, don't baby yourself. In most cases you'll roll better because you'll be feeling better and your mind and body will respond more easily.

"With common sense, preventive maintenance and ultilization of all possible aids, there's no reason why any bowler can't go on and on."

A TIP FROM MIKE LEMONGELLO

"Keeping your bowling hand in shape is important to your game. Some bowlers have the mistaken idea that the more they practice the stronger their hand will become. This isn't true. I find that my practices varies. Sometimes I roll two games, sometimes ten and sometimes as many as forty in a day. I roll only enough to give me the stroke and the looseness I need. Every bowler must work to find when he's had enough practice and at what point he's just wasting his time and straining his hand.

"Your whole game, your mental attitude, and everything else can be just great, but if your hand is bad and you can't do what you want, your game is shot. Roll enough games so that your hand develops the strength you need. Then roll enough to keep your hand and your game in shape without serious problems."

26

FOR THE SENIORS

At eighty-two Andy Varipapa was still instructing, giving exhibitions and averaging better than 180. At sixty-two Buzz Fazio was still rolling for big money on the pro tour.

This pair of Hall of Famers are typical of the senior citizens who enjoy bowling, and can enjoy it at any age. Varipapa claims that if you can move you can bowl.

But even a physical marvel like Fazio advises that bowlers concede a bit to the passing years.

BUZZ FAZIO

"When a bowler is at that fifty or older mark he must learn to pace himself, relax both body and mind, and watch the diet a little closer.

"As you get older, you don't have the speed and coordination you had when you were younger. Do everything the same but shorten your steps and go to a lighter ball. As time goes on, arm strength diminishes slightly. But an older bowler should be careful not to cut the arm swing. A normal, fluid swing will keep the ball rolling.

"To help get that roll, make sure you don't pitch the ball. You can reach past the foul line as long as you're not standing erect. If you have trouble bending at the knee, bend from the waist.

"An older bowler shouldn't bother himself with special lines used by the pros and he shouldn't attempt to work the ball too much. Let the ball roll off the fingers. Work within your style, but don't get fancy. Go the other way, concentrate more on the basics of approach and ball release. Use your energy where it's needed most."

27

ABOUT LEFTIES

Some of the greatest bowlers in the world—Johnny Petraglia, Dave Davis, Mike McGrath, Don Glover, Skee Foremsky, Butch Gearhart, Don Helling, Larry Lichstein, Marty Piraino and Bill Allen—are left-handed.

There was a time when you started from the bottom of a prize list to find the southpaws.

In the early days the track was an advantage. Thus the fact that the left side of the lane was little used and there was no track there proved to be a huge disadvantage for the lefties.

The cliché most often accepted about left-handed bowlers was that they all rolled big hooks and were wild, like the fabled baseball pitchers who had worlds of stuff but didn't know how to get the ball over the plate.

Allen explains why most southpaws, not all, do roll big hooks, "Most of them hook the ball easily because they start from the extreme left of the lane. That's the simplest and best angle for a lefty to play because it gives a true roll and stronger finishing ball.

"The lefty doesn't have to worry about the track problems a righty might have because his side of the lane doesn't have any track. A lefty has more leeway when it comes to spot bowling for the same reason. If he's loose he has a wide pocket practically all the time.

"Lefties don't normally have to worry about playing two or three different angles, sometimes in the same day. They usually have a cleaner and truer surface and should be able to build great confidence because

ON GLOVER

SKEE FOREMSKY

TCH GEARHART

BILL ALLEN

if they roll it the same way, it will do the same thing almost all the time. That isn't always true for the righties.

"The tour advantage to lefties is moneywise, not pinwise. When a house is good for lefties, each lefty has only a dozen or less men to beat. If the center is high-scoring for righties, there are at least fifty tigers to beat."

All basic fundamentals in bowling apply the same to left-handers as they do to right-handers. The lefty must always be mindful that he is rolling on practically a new lane all the time. He can't follow a track and usually there isn't another left-hander around for him to follow.

28

TALL BOWLERS

The major fault of tall bowlers, says supertall (6–4) superpro Dave Soutar, is their habit of raising up when they're at the foul line.

"If you're not low when you reach the foul line the ball bangs into the lane and you can't roll it smoothly. Tall bowlers have long legs which usually means long steps which usually means poor timing. That doesn't help good bowling."

This can be overcome by taking short steps at the start and concentrating on being close to the floor at the end of the approach. Another problem of tall bowlers is speed. Most tall bowlers build up speed without any extra effort.

Soutar warns, "The way the ball hits is your clue to speed. When the ball hits flat and doesn't mix, you know you're too fast. The correction here is to hold the ball low. With the body erect and the ball held low at the start, it's difficult to swing too far back, the cause of the speed."

There are great advantages in being tall and they more than compensate for the problems.

Adds Soutar, "A tall bowler can reach far out when releasing the ball and his longer arms make it easier for him to get the ball a good way down the lane before it starts rolling. The key pendulum swing is much easier for the tall bowler, and though speed can be a detriment, it's also nice to know that the taller bowler can gain speed easily when lane conditions call for it."

29

WOMEN'S BOWLING

Almost as many women as men roll these days, and well too. One of the greatest women bowlers of all time, Sylvia Wene, stands a mere 4–11. Dotty Fothergill, twice Bowler of the Year, is just about 5 feet tall and weighs slightly more than 100 pounds. There are many other examples of female bowlers, petite and feminine, who average much higher than the pro men's par of 200.

So for the average bowler it is obvious that physical prowess is not all-important. As Frank Clause, longtime professional instructor, noted to thousands of women during his clinics, "Bowling is more a game of brains than brawn once you have a smooth delivery and learn where to place the ball."

Women normally have better balance than men and can learn to get to the line more smoothly. A disadvantage is the simple fact that women just aren't as physically strong as men, so they should avoid those aspects of the game where physical strength comes into play.

First, the weight of the ball should be considered very carefully. A woman shouldn't roll with a ball much over 14 pounds unless it is extremely comfortable to her. Women, unless they're in the professional class, shouldn't attempt to develop large, sharp-breaking hooks. The natural construction of a women's arm is such that a free swing would tend to give her a straight ball or even a backup. Thus a large hook for the average woman bowler would probably cause a little too much strain.

But there is no reason why any woman, regardless of size or age, can't roll a short hook. It will take some extra practice to keep the hand position so that the thumb is at ten o'clock, but a little extra practice and determination will do it.

Most women roll the ball too slowly simply because their backswing is short, which is simply the result of a too short pushaway.

Women should also try pressing down with the index finger and the pinky. This will keep the other fingers firmly in the ball and help keep the wrist straight. At ball release women particularly should make sure they reach for a spot or pins, keep the arm straight and then reach for the roof. Exaggerate the hook position if necessary to nine o'clock.

In all other ways the basic fundamentals of bowling remain the same for men and women. The average man in a league averages 155 or thereabouts, while the average woman is around the 130 to 132 mark, a difference of about 25 pins.

30

CHILDREN AND BOWLING

Bowling is more and more getting to be a kid's game. Youngsters under five years of age bowl, and some pre-teeners make Mom and Dad sit up and take notice, and lumps, when the family goes bowling together. Teenagers have become full-fledged pros and have won major titles.

However, when it comes to children, it should be a fun game all the way.

Just as soon as a youngster is able to push or shove the ball down a lane he should be allowed to bowl. Again, fun is the main thing. Don't even attempt to teach a small youngster anything beyond putting the proper fingers in the ball and getting to the line without falling.

One of the innate urges of the human animal is to throw things. Another is to destroy set patterns. All our lives, particularly as youngsters, we're told not to touch things, not to step on the grass, not to throw things. All at once bowling gives a youngster a new world. Let him go. He won't be strong enough to do any damage as long as you keep within the confines of the lane.

In the next phase the small youngster will tire of his newfound fun and freedom because maybe he isn't knocking the pins down too well. Now is the time for some simple, basic instruction.

Point out the various markers on the approach and lane, but do it casually, and don't expect too much. Let the youngster feel his way. You'll be amazed what a difference a few outings will make.

The worst thing parents and coaches can do is to insist on and force

youngsters to do anything except stay within the bounds of safety, courtesy and common sense.

When a child begins to respond by asking questions, by getting a little mad at things, he's beginning to get hooked a little. Unless a youngster likes bowling, he won't want to learn too much past the idea of being able to throw the ball. If that's the case, let him be.

If he wants to learn more, help. Make sure he has the proper equipment. Carefully select the proper junior leagues with the proper organization and administration, and guide him. Don't boss a young bowler and don't let him boss you.

Ages are unimportant. Some youngsters are ready physically and mentally at five years old. Some teenagers couldn't care less. The young bowler is usually eager to learn, but short on patience. He's in a hurry to become the next Don Johnson. Slow him down. Bowling should be second to school at all times. It should never be allowed to interfere.

All young bowlers who manage to get a few strikes in a row and rack up a few good games have illusions of grandeur and how great it would be to be a pro winning all that money on TV.

It's up to the parents and coaches to put bowling in its proper perspective, as a good wholesome outlet. Too often, it's the parents who push too much.

Future pros will make their future. They will carve their own way by bowling as much as they can, by learning through watching, talking and reading.

There is specialty equipment for young bowlers—balls, bags, shoes and all other accessories. Never push a child bowler. Never expose him to any portion of bowling that is either physically or mentally too taxing. They should be treated the same as any other bowlers, with the addition of a little tact and a lot more caring.

31

PRESSURE AND THE MENTAL SIDE OF BOWLING

Bowling is a fun game, but it's also a competitive game. Competition is conflict, and where there's conflict, there's pressure. Whether it's that single game for a cup of coffee or that single game for a $25,000 prize, pressure is there.

It's been said a thousand times by the finest and most talented athletes in every field of sport, and for that matter by talented people in other fields, that you never get used to pressure.

Don't let outward appearances fool you. Tension grips the most seasoned performer. That doesn't necessarily mean it reduces ability. Some rise to their greatest heights when under the most pressure.

You must live with pressure, like or not. The first step in the battle against pressure is to admit it is there and won't silently slip away. Each individual must battle pressure in his own way.

You become good at something the same way you learn to ice skate: you keep making a fool of yourself until you master it. Good judgment comes from experience, and experience comes from the results of bad judgment. Money can't buy experience.

The veteran performers, having been through pressure-packed situations so often, have developed combat weapons. All agree that a deep breath before a key shot invariably helps and that full concentration on what you're doing, not on what it means or who is watching, is the most important thing.

Some chew gum or tobacco. Others fidget, using excess movement to get rid of excess energy built up by the adrenaline pouring into the bloodstream. Some talk more, others talk less.

Look in the mirror. If you don't know the best way to calm the person looking back at you, start thinking about it. Don't think you're all alone because a triple gets you nervous or you shake when you face a spare in a crucial moment.

"Too many bowlers say they can't, and they don't," says Lou Scalia. "Try mental imaging which is simply positive thinking. Look at yourself at your best, not your worst. Don't picture the ten pin standing, picture it blowing out of there."

Dick Ritger advises, "In the clutch make a decision and live with it. Some bowlers shoot for a pack [solid pocket hit] strike in the clutch while others aim for a wider pocket, just trying to be loose with the shot. Neither is right or wrong. Just stay with whatever you decide and that alone will relax you."

Bob Strampe says, "Take inventory, block out the crowd, and take a cool walk to the line. If you're afraid panic is going to get you, dream up a big panic button. Just knowing it's there when you need it will reassure you that you don't need it."

"When you have a pressure situation," adds Mike McGrath, "it's simply a matter of execution. You've made strikes thousands of times, you have shot at every conceivable spare. Just think about how many times you have shot them—and made them."

Billy Hardwick and Bill Allen, two of the finest clutch bowlers ever, feel that the chance to win should override thoughts of pressure. "You only have so many opportunities in life. You've got to grab them," says Allen.

Hardwick advises not to try to be too perfect. "Just try to make a good shot. If you try to be perfect you won't do things the way you normally do."

Don Russell probably sums up all the different methods of beating pressure best when he says, "The sure way to rid yourself of pressure is to become as sure as you can of your game."

Probably the most pressure a bowler can face is the tension of bowling in competition on television. These days there are many local shows featuring average bowlers in addition to the nationally televised events starring the top pros.

Here you have the same pressure of a crucial situation plus the added heat of the lights, the movement of cameras and equipment, plus the horrifying thought that millions of people are watching you.

You must erase those people out there, if the thought of them bothers you. On the other hand, TV often brings out the ham in bowlers, and they want to show their ability in this greatest of all showcases. Either way, it gets back to individual personalities.

If you do have the opportunity to roll on TV, be prepared for a bit of extra perspiration. Be ready for unusual breaks in the game for commercials. Be prepared for possible movements from the side of the lane or from TV technicians who are so busy with their own end of the production that they fail to realize how much a bowler must concentrate. But that's the key: concentrate so hard on your game that if someone fell in front of you all it would mean would be an extra hop in your delivery.

Remember, pressure is a normal part of the game, and feeling it is also a normal human reaction. Face it the best way you know how. Maybe Winston Churchill's experience works best. He said, "It is very much better to have a panic feeling beforehand, and then be quite calm when things happen, than to be extremely calm beforehand and to get into a panic when things happen."

A TIP FROM TIM HARAHAN

"Most young bowlers roll scared. A youngster moving up to a better league or going out on tour often looks up too much to the stars. He worries and wonders so much that his own concentration causes his game to suffer.

"Up and coming bowlers have a natural inclination to change too quickly. Bowlers should be ready to make changes, but only after they have had enough experience. Young bowlers changing right away run into trouble.

"Make a change when necessary, but don't make a change just for the sake of making a change, and never because you see other bowlers doing it."

32

LEAGUE BOWLING

The competitive aspect of bowling is one of its many lures, and the beauty of bowling is that any bowler of any ability level, either sex, with only the oddest hours to spare, can engage in league play.

Too many bowlers feel that they just aren't good enough for league play. Nothing could be farther from the truth. Whether you're a 75-average beginner or 200-plus-average pro, there's a spot for you.

Some eight million people—men, women and children—roll in leagues sanctioned by the American Bowling Congress, Women's International Bowling Congress and American Junior Bowling Congress. A league is simply organized competition, usually based on five bowlers to a team. But there are also four, three and two man and women teams as well as mixed leagues. Participation in the latter has been increasing with each passing year, and mixed leagues now make up about half of all the leagues.

Any group can form a league. Many leagues are made up of people who work for the same firm or in the same industry; others are out-growths of clubs, religious groups, or some other organized group or just a group of people who like bowling and have been organized for that purpose.

Every bowling center forms its own leagues, called house leagues. They are formed with every type bowler in mind, from the housewife who rolls at 9:00 A.M. to the late-shift worker who may start his bowling after midnight.

Since bowlers have wide-ranging degrees of skill, leagues must equalize the competition. This is done by handicapping, awarding the lower-average bowler enough pins to bring him up to standards set by the league. Handicaps are designed to bring all bowlers as close together as possible.

Over the years, handicapping each individual bowler, whether the bowler is rolling individually or as part of a team, has proven to be the best method.

A base or scratch score is determined, usually 200, but sometimes as low as 180 or as high as 220. Then a decision is made as to what percentage of the difference between the bowler's average and the scratch score will be used. This ranges from as low as 50 percent to a full 100 percent, with the trend being nearer 100 percent. A low is usually established. For instance, a male may not receive handicap on an average of less than 140 and a female less than 120. If their averages fall below those figures, they must take the figure set as the low.

For any person interested in the organizational phase of a league, materials are available from most bowling centers or from the ABC, WIBC and National Bowling Council. Rules, organization, handicap manuals and anything else needed to form and to operate a league are easy to obtain. The same is true for tournaments, often called the icing on bowling's competitive cake.

Bowling in a league brings new dimensions to the bowler. He becomes more interested because he becomes more involved. Every bowler should join a league as quickly as possible.

A TIP FROM LES ZIKES

"Bowling is a real and continuing challenge, and if you don't accept the challenge to improve, you're missing much of what the game has to offer. Intelligent practice is the way to meet the challenge—but practice, don't just throw the ball.

"A practice session is the place to try a new ball, a new stance or new approach, and it's the place to better your skill with a line you don't ordinarily use. Practice is what helps the beginner hit the headpin with better consistency.

"Some pros practice more in one week than the average bowler does in a year, yet some of them, in fact many of them, practice only three or six games at a clip. That's well within the reach of any bowler.

"Make the most of the practice time you have. Using a buddy, teammate, local pro or anyone else you feel is capable to advise you about your weak spots and how to correct them, learn what area of your game needs the work. Then practice, whether it's one or 100 games. Gear your practice to your own game, your own personality, your own temperament. Much of your improvement and success will be in direct proportion to the amount and kind of practice you do.

"Take a page from our serious bowlers overseas. They make time for practice. In Japan people who can afford to roll only a single game often make reservations to roll that one lonesome game before they go to work in the morning.

"Remember, your score in practice is the least important thing, but practice will lead to the all-important higher scores where they count most."

33

EVERYTHING YOU WANTED TO KNOW ABOUT BOWLING— AND HAVE ASKED

Bowling, even on the professional level, is one of the most informal sports ever devised. The spectator is within a few feet of the competitor. Bowlers are known by sight to the interested fans. Between sessions, bowlers often talk to the spectators and answer all types of questions. Some questions are asked over and over again. Others are specific questions about a specific bowler's game. Following are some of the most interesting as judged by the bowlers and officials who had to answer them. They cover a wide range, from rules and regulations through advanced instructional techniques to some that might be considered personal and private. Read them. Your question might be there. In any case, you will learn a great deal more about bowlers and bowling.

Question. What is a touring pro?
Answer. Like any membership organization of the same type, the Professional Bowlers Association has various designations. A touring pro I is a

player who has participated in two thirds (66.67 percent) of the tournaments held in the previous calendar year or a bowler who was among the leading 25 money winners.

A touring pro II is a player who participated in half (50 percent) of the tournaments staged the previous year.

Other categories are resident pros I and II, apprentice, inactive, retired and associate pros. Basically the touring pro is the player who makes his living by bowling in competition. The resident pro is the home pro, a pro who is involved in either a pro shop business or an allied field and rolls in only a few tournaments each year on the national tour, but rolls extensively in regional and weekend events.

Q. What is a pro-am?

A. Preceding almost every pro tournament is the pro-am tournament, competition that pairs amateurs of any average with pros. The usual format is for each amateur to roll three games on the same pair of lanes while the pros move after each game. This would give each amateur the opportunity to roll with three different pros. The final score is the score of the amateur, the scores of the pros and the amateur's handicap all added together. A pro-am combines the fun and excitement of rolling with the world's best, gaining a few on-the-spot tips, and also having a chance to win prizes in competition.

Q. I roll a backup and just can't seem to be able to switch to a straight ball or a hook, even though I understand that the hand position with the thumb to the left will do it. I just don't feel comfortable. Can't I live with the backup?

A. Yes you can. Listen to New York lefty pro Dick Battista who advises, "If you're a right-hander and you're comfortable with a backup, stay with it but then roll the ball from the left side of the lane into the 1–2 pocket. It will be the same as a hook then, a left-hander's hook."

Q. My thumb sometime swells when I bowl a few games. Don't the pros have the same trouble?

A. Pros have a very simple method to overcome the swelling thumb. Most have the thumb hole drilled larger than necessary. Then they line it with any number of strips of thin tape, usually the electrical type. As the thumb swells, they simply remove as many strips of tape as necessary to maintain the feel and size they want. Often you will see a pro bowler taking or putting something on the bottom of his bowling shoe. Actually, the spot directly in front of the heel, since it never touches the floor, is a good storing site for the strips of tape while bowling. No worry about

DICK BATTISTA

leaving a roll of tape lying around, and strips can be precut to the proper size before bowling.

Q. What's the more difficult feat, a hole in one in golf or a 300 game in bowling?

A. This question is asked very often. Golf is the favorite second sport of pro bowlers, and a number of them, Buzz Fazio, Jim Stefanich, Billy Welu and Bill Johnson, could have taken either sport as a pro career. As to which feat is more difficult, the consensus of bowler-golfers who have achieved both makes sense. A hole in one takes one stroke. A 300 game takes 12 strikes. One lucky stroke comes far more often than 12 lucky strikes.

Q. Can bowling be practiced at home?

A. All parts of the approach and delivery can be practiced at home. An iron can serve as a bowling ball, or better yet, prop up an old cushion in a corner and you can also practice ball release. One big advantage of home practice is the opportunity to utilize a mirror to check out certain positions.

Q. What is the explosion point?

A. This is the split-second segment at ball release when your thumb has left the ball and it rests on the fingers. It is at this point you apply the lift. The lift, stuff or action applied here will determine how well the ball will act against the pins a few seconds later. It might be better called the fuse lighting point, which leads to the explosion later.

Q. What happens if the pins are slightly off spot?

A. Pin action depends on each pin of the ten-pin setup doing its job. If one pin is off it won't bounce or react the way it should and the result is bad pinfall. If a pin is obviously off spot enough to cause a problem, rerack. If a certain pin remains far off spot, then the bowling proprietor should be informed so he can correct it at his first chance.

Q. Where does the prize money in a tournament come from?

A. In pro tournaments it usually comes from three sources: the entry fees put up by the participating bowlers, from the host bowling center, and from commercial sponsors. The larger the field, the more the money. For every three entries there is at least one prize in the pro ranks. In nonpro tournaments the ratio is usually one prize for ten entries, and seldom is there any added money.

Q. My fingers are sore and aching when I finish bowling. I've had my ball checked and the fit is okay. I don't bowl too many games at one time. What else could cause this problem?

A. When excessive effort is used on the backswing, there is also a tendency to add pull to the ball as it comes down and forward prior to release. When this happens the normal weight of the ball is increased due to the momentum and could have the effect of ten or more times its weight. If a bowler attempts to apply the lift at this point the tremendous force is too much for the fingers and the result is sore and aching fingers. The cure is to cut down the speed of the body and the effort of the arm.

Also, the ball must be lifted with the flats of the fingers (the opposite sides to the fingernails). If you attempt to lift with the sides of the fingers, the ball weight will be too much and cause aches and pains.

Q. Do all the stars take four or five steps?

A. Four is the most popular approach to the line, then five. However, there have been noteworthy exceptions. The fabled Count Gengler took one step. Adolph Carlson was a two-step bowler. Lee Jouglard and Tony Sparando are three-steppers. Stan Gifford looked like he took about ten tiny steps to the line, and the man who won the first pro tourney ever staged, Lou Campi, finished on the wrong foot. All the unorthodox bowlers would be the first to tell you to do what they say, not what they do.

Q. When adjusting to lane conditions, is it better to move the body or the spot?

A. It is usually better to change the spot. If your ball is crossing the headpin simply select a spot more to the right. If the ball isn't coming up to the headpin, then choose a spot more to the left. However, if the lane condition is extreme, either hooking to excess or not hooking at all, then you should also move your body to compensate. Always move your body to the left to overcome a hooking condition and to the right to combat a slick or nonhooking condition. More speed and getting the ball out on the lane a greater distance will also help hold the line on a hooking condition, while a slower ball not tossed out as far will aid you on the nonhooking condition.

Q. Do bowlers follow any special diet?

A. Because pro bowlers must roll at odd hours of the day, they learn to eat different meals at different times from the norm, as is true with most athletes. No bowler should eat a heavy meal just before bowling. The top bowlers are in good physical shape. Over the years a look at the top twenty money winners each year will show that at least fifteen are on the thin side.

Q. Is there any difference between a colored ball and a plain black ball?

A. Because of certain differences in the manufacturing end, a black ball will grip a little more in most cases. It is only in recent years that many better bowlers began to use a wide variety of colored balls. If you see a color you like, don't hesitate. One advantage is that it's much easier to locate your ball on the rack.

Q. I'm undecided as to whether I should take a whack at pro bowling when I graduate from high school or go on to college and try bowling later. What are the pros and cons?

A. At your age (late teens probably) there is no doubt that you should go on to college. You can still bowl while in college and pick up some added experience. Much of bowling is mental, and if college increases your ability to think and adds poise, it will help your bowling game. And finally, pro bowling is a gamble and even the top stars don't last forever, so a college degree with at least the basic background in some field will serve as a backup insofar as earning a living is concerned.

Q. Everyone emphasizes that the backswing shouldn't go higher than the shoulder. How about those with shorter backswings? Is there a low limit too?

A. It's not a question of limits. Unless the backswing goes to at least the waist-high level, it's unlikely the bowler will be able to build up enough momentum. So let's say that the backswing should be at least waist-high and no higher than the shoulder to achieve the best results.

Q. I thought I saw a bowler with a four-finger ball. Is this possible?

A. Possible and probable. Bowlers have used balls with holes from no fingers to all five. Unless there is a physical problem, such grips usually do more harm than help. When you go to either of the extremes you have either too much grip or not enough.

Q. I feel that my approach is consistent, I hit my spot well, and yet my ball is inconsistent. Any suggestions?

A. Could be your lift. Varying degrees of lift will cause the ball to react differently. One important fact to remember is to never apply lift until your ball has passed your left foot during the final step of your delivery. This is the beginning of the upswing.

Q. I would like to bowl more, but I'm limited to once a week. Do you have any special advice for me?

A. First, don't expect too much in the way of average, so don't become discouraged if your progress is slow. Don't try to put too much stuff on the ball, settle for a slight hook. Develop as easy an approach and as easy a ball release as possible. Concentrate on hitting the headpin.

Q. I saw Carmen Salvino win a tournament on television and he had no style at all. The ball was limp at his side, hanging like a weight. Should I try styles like that?

A. Salvino is an old pro. The style eliminated his pushaway and gave him a grooved swing. It worked for him because he is physically strong and had the patience needed to practice this unique style. If you're strong and have patience, try it. For most bowlers, it is not advisable.

Q. What about bowling slumps? How do you avoid them?

A. Bowling has the longest season of all sports, so slumps are inevitable. Frank Clause always advised, "Keep thinking all the time. You can't go through the same motions exactly the same way every time you bowl because you're not the same person. You're stronger, you're weaker. Just stick with it." Pros break slumps by breaking their game apart and checking each part. Then they bowl more to get out of it, or bowl less to get a rest.

Q. There are no pros where I live. How can I get good instruction?

A. It's often been said that for each bowler there are at least two instructors. Actually, you don't have to be a good bowler to be a good instructor. Any person, man or woman, who is interested enough in the game to get to know the game and its basics can be a good instructor. Preferably, the instructor should know your game or be willing to watch you enough to know your game. But remember, the one thing worse than no instructor is two instructors at the same time.

Q. My thumb is oddly shaped. Can't I get a ball drilled to fit it?

A. Of course. No finger or thumb is perfectly round. They're tapered, knobby and anything but perfect. One of the many mysteries of life is why thumb holes are drilled round. A bowler should work on his ball, using a knife and sandpaper to make the hole wide where the thumb is wide. The thumb should be comfortable, yet snug if possible. Your best bet is to have the thumb drilled small, then work it out to fit your particular thumb. If any bowler feels his thumb or fingers need special drilling attention, a pro will be happy to show you how to do it, or to do it for you.

Q. I keep hearing about revolutions on the ball. Is this important?

A. It's vital to a working ball. The number of revolution isn't as important as the number of revolutions left on the ball after it skids. A good working ball will skid and roll 40 feet and then hook and turn for the final 20 feet. Too fast and the ball will turn only the final 5 feet, and even then it's still in a semiskid and won't carry. If the ball is too slow the revolutions start coming off 30 feet from the pins, and by the time the ball gets there it is spent or flat, leaving the 5 pin or a 5–7 or 8–10 split.

Revolutions are imparted to the ball with finger lift at the ball release or explosion point. This, plus the amount of resistance the ball encounters on the lane (oil, dressing, etc.), will actually determine the number of revolutions. There can be as few as 5 or less, as many as 15. The idea is to be able to control the ball so that 8 to 10 revolutions are there just before the ball hits the pins.

Q. Are pro bowlers superstitious?

A. No more or less than other athletes. If they roll well with a certain pair of slacks or shirt, they'll continue to use them. And one bowler who swears he is not superstitious claims it's a scientific fact that when he wears something red he bowls better.

Q. How can I tell if my armswing is straight?

A. Fold a towel under your arm. Then swing your arm back and forth. If the towel falls, your arm isn't moving in a straight line. You can practice at home until that towel stays; then you know the swing has the proper arc.

Q. Why is it that some of the pros don't watch their opponents bowl?

A. Dave Davis is a prime example. Dave's explanation is that he wants to bowl his own game. He doesn't want to see his opponent get a lucky hit which might be upsetting.

Q. What is playing safe?

A. Playing safe is a term applied to a bowler who, needing a strike or spare in the last frame, elects to miss the headpin to avoid a split and leave an easy spare. For better bowlers there is no such thing. Too often a bowler leaves a difficult spare. The right way to play safe when you need a mark is to go for a strike.

Don Johnson comments, "You can't play safe if you want to make it. You've got to be a gambler. I've moved my angle as much as 15 to 20 boards in the same day, sometimes in the same game. Most of the time the changes have earned me more money than I would have won if I tried to play it safe, whatever that means."

Q. Do bowlers vary the weight of the ball? Should they?

A. Al Thompson often practices with a light ball, then uses a heavier one in competition. "Most of us roll the ball too fast," says Al. My method slows you down because in competition the ball is heavier and you roll it better." Once, after practicing with a 12-pounder, Thompson appeared on TV and rolled a 300 game with a 16-pounder.

Q. What kind of goals should a bowler set?

A. Depends on what the bowler is after. If it's just fun, there are no goals. If it's to improve and move on to better competition, then the goals must be realistic. It's not difficult to be a 150 bowler. A little more work and 170 comes fairly easy. But once past the 180 mark the going gets tougher, and then it's a matter of adding knowledge, practicing more, building up patience, and learning all the time, not just when you're in the right mood.

One question asked by a little girl must go unanswered. In all sincerity she asked, "What kind of bowling ball does God use?"

This section should encourage you not to hesitate to ask better bowlers and the top pros questions about the game, yours, theirs, anyone's. They will do their best to help.

Rules, Regulations and the
American Bowling Congress

Throughout this book many of the rules of bowling have been mentioned. Here are additional selected playing rules which every bowler should be well aware of, rules that most often must be consulted.

Legal Pinfall

Every ball delivered by the player shall count, unless declared a dead ball. Pins must then be respotted after the cause for declaring such dead ball has been removed.

Pins which are knocked down by another pin or pins rebounding in play from the side partition, rear cushion or sweep bar when it is at rest on the pin deck prior to sweeping dead wood are counted as pins down.

If when rolling at a full setup or in order to make a spare, it is discovered immediately after the ball has been delivered that one or more pins are improperly set, although not missing, the ball and resulting pinfall shall be counted. It is each player's responsibility to determine if the setup is correct. He shall insist that any pins incorrectly set be respotted before delivering his ball; otherwise he implies that the setup is satisfactory. No change in the position of any pins which are left standing can be made after a previous delivery in order to make a spare, unless the pinsetter has moved or misplaced any pin after the previous delivery and prior to the bowling of the next ball.

Pins which are knocked down by a fair ball, and remain lying on the lane or in the gutters, or which lean so as to touch kickbacks or side partitions, are termed dead wood and counted as pins down, and must be removed before the next ball is bowled.

Illegal Pinfall

When any of the following incidents occur the ball counts as a ball rolled, but pins knocked down shall not count:

When pins are knocked down or displaced by a ball which leaves the lane before reaching the pins.

When a ball rebounds from the rear cushion.

When pins come in contact with the body, arms or legs of a human pinsetter and rebound.

A standing pin which falls when it is touched by mechanical pinsetting equipment, or when dead wood is removed, or is knocked down by a human pinsetter, shall not count and must be replaced on the pin spot inscribed on the pin deck where it originally stood before delivery of the ball.

Pins which are bowled off the lane, rebound and remain standing on the lane must be counted as pins standing.

If in delivering the ball a foul is committed, any pins knocked down by such delivery shall not be counted.

Dead Ball

A ball shall be declared dead if any of the following occur, in which case such ball shall not count. The pins must be respotted after the cause for declaring such dead ball has been removed and player shall be required to rebowl.

If after the player delivers his ball attention is immediately called to the fact that one or more pins were missing from the setup.

When a human pinsetter removes or interferes with any pin or pins before they stop rolling or before the ball reaches the pins.

When a player bowls on the wrong lane or out of turn.

When a player is interfered with by a pinsetter, another bowler, spectator, or moving object as the ball is being delivered and before delivery is completed, player must then and there accept the resulting pinfall or demand that pins be respotted.

When any pins at which he is bowling are moved or knocked down in any manner as the player is delivering the ball and before the ball reaches the pins.

When a player's ball comes in contact with any foreign obstacle.

Balls—Private Ownership

Bowling balls used in the game and marked by their owners are considered private, and other participants in the game are prohibited from using the same, unless the owner consents to such use.

Foul

A foul is committed with no pinfall being credited to the player, although the ball counts as a ball rolled, when a part of the bowler's person encroaches upon or goes beyond the foul line and touches any part of the lane, equipment or building during or after executing a legal delivery. A ball is in play and a foul may be called after legal delivery has been made and until the same or another player is on the approach in position to make a succeeding delivery.

If the player commits a foul which is apparent to both captains or one or more members of the opposing teams competing in a league or tournament on the same pair of lanes where the foul is committed, or to the official scorer or a tournament official, and should the foul judge or umpire through negligence fail to see it committed or an ABC approved automatic foul detecting device fail to record it, a foul shall nevertheless be declared and so recorded.

Deliberate Foul

If a player deliberately fouls to benefit by the calling of a foul, he shall be immediately disqualified from further participation in the series then in play and his place may be taken by another player. The deliberate foul shall not be allowed.

A player who willfully throws his ball into the gutter shall be immediately removed from the game and series and his place may be taken by another player.

If no substitute is available to take the place of the removed player, his team shall be credited only with the pins knocked down up to the time the player was disqualified plus one tenth of his blind score for each of the remaining frames in the game.

Foul Counts as Ball Bowled

A foul ball shall be recorded as a ball bowled by the player, but any pins bowled down when a foul is committed shall not count. When the player fouls upon delivering the first ball of a frame, all pins knocked down must be respotted, and only those pins knocked down by the second ball may be counted. If he bowls down all the pins with his second ball after fouling with the first, it shall be scored as a spare. When less than ten pins are bowled down on the second ball after fouling on the first, it shall be scored as an error. A player who fouls when delivering his second ball of a frame shall be credited with only those pins bowled down with his first ball, provided no foul was committed when the first ball was delivered. When a bowler fouls during the delivery of his first ball in the tenth frame and bowls down all ten pins with his second ball (making a spare) he bowls a third ball and is credited with a spare plus the pins bowled down with the third ball. When a player fouls while delivering his third ball in the tenth frame, only those pins bowled down in delivering his first two balls shall be counted.

No Unreasonable Delay

The league or tournament officials shall allow no unreasonable delay in the progress of any game. Should any member or team participating in a league or tournament refuse to proceed with the game after being directed to do so by the proper authorities, such game or series shall be declared forfeited.

Foul—Detection

League and tournament officials may adopt and use any ABC approved automatic foul detecting device, and where none is available a foul judge must be stationed so he has an unobstructed view of the foul line.

Penalty for Unfair Tactics

Any member of the American Bowling Congress violating the provisions of this rule as outlined below shall be liable for the penalties indicated, and anyone who is not a member of the Congress but who has violated the provisions of this rule shall be refused membership in the Congress until the Board of Directors of the Congress approves his application.

a. Attempting to gain an unfair advantage.

1. By directly or indirectly tampering with lanes, bowling pins and/or bowling balls so they no longer meet ABC specifications.

2. By misrepresenting an average either to gain a greater handicap or to qualify for a lower classification in a sanctioned league or tournament.

3. By establishing an average below his ability and thereby gaining an unfair advantage in handicap or classified competition.

Penalty—loss of game or games including prize winnings and/or suspension of membership where unfair advantage was secured.

b. Placing the game of tenpins in jeopardy of unfair criticism by the use of dishonest or disreputable tactics in connection with the game of bowling. Penalty—suspension of membership.

c. Failing to distribute team prize money in accordance with verbal or written agreements. Penalty—suspension of membership.

d. Failing to pay fees due for participation in a sanctioned league or tournament. Penalty—suspension of membership.

Gambling—Pool—Lottery

No bowling proprietor shall allow on his premises handbooks, pools or any schemes of gambling nature to be made or handled involving the outcome of bowling games, whether the bowling games be sanctioned league or tournament play. Failure to terminate such gambling practices in his establishments, or any part thereof, when such practices are within his knowledge or when he shall have been notified of same shall be cause for such violations being called to the attention of the local association officers.

The following are the requirements which must be met for eligibility for ABC high score awards:

The high score must have been bowled in a league or tournament sanctioned by the American Bowling Congress.

The lanes upon which the score was bowled must have been certified by the American Bowling Congress for the current season prior to the bowling of the high score game.

A competent foul judge or an automatic foul detecting device approved by the American Bowling Congress must have been employed during the full time the score was being bowled.

Every provision of the ABC constitution, rules and regulations must have been in effect by those conducting the league or tournament in which the high score was bowled.

Notification of the high score must be given to the local association secretary within 24 hours after it has been bowled. This notification must be given by the league or tournament secretary.

No more than fourteen (14) days may elapse before the local association secretary or president gives such notification to the Executive Secretary-Treasurer of the American Bowling Congress.

The secretary of the local association or his duly authorized representative must inspect and measure the lanes on which the score was bowled, and inspect and weigh the very pins used when the high score was bowled. These pins should be set aside in a receptacle immediately after conclusion of the series and sealed in the presence of the two opposing team captains awaiting their inspection and weighing by the local association secretary or his duly authorized representative. This inspection and weighing together with the examination of the lanes must be done within 72 hours after the score has been rolled. He must submit his completed report or affidavit to the American Bowling Congress, setting forth his recommendation for approval or rejection of the claim. The report signed by opposing captains or players, foul judge, official scorer, league or tournament secretary, together with the original score sheet, or a true copy of the original score sheet, must reach the office of the American Bowling Congress before thirty days have elapsed.

When claims for recognition of individual high games of 300, 299, and 298 are submitted, the Executive Secretary-Treasurer of the American Bowling Congress may approve the issuance of the award immediately upon receipt of the evidence and affidavits required, or he may refer claims to the ABC Board of Directors and delegates for their consideration.

APPENDIX 2

Bowling Statistics, Awards and Championships

BOWLING WRITERS ASSOCIATION OF AMERICA BOWLER OF THE YEAR AWARD

1942—Johnny Crimmins,
   Detroit, Mich.
1943—Ned Day, Milwaukee, Wis.
1944—Ned Day, Milwaukee, Wis.
1945—Buddy Bomar, Chicago, Ill.
1946—Joe Wilman, Chicago, Ill.
1947—Buddy Bomar, Chicago, Ill.
1948—Andy Varipapa, Brooklyn, N.Y.
1949—Connie Schwoegler,
   Madison, Wis.
1950—Junie McMahon,
   Fair Lawn, N.J.
1951—Lee Jouglard, Detroit, Mich.
1952—Steve Nagy, Cleveland, Ohio
1953—Don Carter, St. Louis, Mo.
1954—Don Carter, St. Louis, Mo.
1955—Steve Nagy, Detroit, Mich.
1956—Bill Lillard, Chicago, Ill
1957—Don Carter, St. Louis, Mo.

1958—Don Carter, St. Louis, Mo.
1959—Ed Lubanski, Detroit, Mich.
1960—Don Carter, St. Louis, Mo.
1961—Dick Weber, St. Louis, Mo.
1962—Don Carter, St. Louis, Mo.
1963—Dick Weber, St. Louis, Mo.
1964—Billy Hardwick,
   San Mateo, Calif.
1965—Dick Weber, St. Louis, Mo.
1966—Wayne Zahn, Atlanta,. Ga.
1967—Dave Davis, Phoenix, Ariz.
1968—Jim Stefanich, Joliet, Ill.
1969—Billy Hardwick, Louisville, Ky.
1970—Nelson Burton, Jr.,
   St. Louis, Mo.
1971—Don Johnson, Akron, Ohio
1972—Don Johnson, Akron, Ohio
1973   Don McCune, Munster, Ind.
1974—Earl Anthony, Tacoma, Wash.
1975—Earl Anthony, Tacoma, Wash.

THE SPORTING NEWS PBA PLAYER OF THE YEAR AWARD

1963—Billy Hardwick, Louisville, Ky.
1964—Bob Strampe, Detroit, Mich.
1965—Dick Weber, St. Louis, Mo.
1966—Wayne Zahn, Atlanta, Ga.
1967—Dave Davis, Phoenix, Ariz.
1968—Jim Stefanich, Joliet, Ill.
1969—Billy Hardwick, Louisville, Ky.

1970—Nelson Burton, Jr.,
   St. Louis, Mo.
1971—Don Johnson, Akron, Ohio
1972—Don Johnson, Akron, Ohio
1973—Don McCune, Munster, Ind.
1974—Earl Anthony, Tacoma, Wash.
1975—Earl Anthony, Tacoma, Wash.

THE SPORTING NEWS ROOKIE OF THE YEAR AWARD

1964—Jerry McCoy, Ft. Worth, Tex.
1965—Jim Godman, Hayward, Calif.
1966—Bobby Cooper, Dallas, Tex.
1967—Mike Durbin,
    Costa Mesa, Calif.
1968—Bob McGregor, Lubbock, Tex.
1969—Larry Lichstein,
    Windsor Locks, Conn.

1970—Denny Krick, Tacoma, Wash.
1971—Tye Critchlow,
    Claremont, Calif.
1972—Tom Hudson, Akron, Ohio
1973—Steve Neff, Sarasota, Fla.
1974—Cliff McNealy,
    San Lorenzo, Calif.

GEORGE YOUNG HIGH AVERAGE AWARD

George Young was a comparatively young man of forty-nine when he died in 1959 when the PBA was a mere baby. As one who helped in the early days of the fledgling group and a man who was always near the top in any bowling competition, it seemed fitting that the award for the highest average each year be named to honor Young.

This is a coveted award as it denotes a bowler who rolled the best in more than 1,000 games of competition under any and all conditions in all sections of the country. It is a true indication of a bowler's all-round skill.

WINNERS OF THE GEORGE YOUNG MEMORIAL AWARD
(Based on competition in at least half of the PBA tournaments contested)

YEAR NAME	NO. TOURNAMENTS	AVERAGE
1962—Don Carter, St. Louis, Mo.	25	212.844
1963—Billy Hardwick, Louisville, Ky.	26	210.346
1964—Ray Bluth, St. Louis, Mo.	27	210.512
1965—Dick Weber, St. Louis, Mo.	19	211.895
1966—Wayne Zahn, Atlanta, Ga.	27	208.663
1967—Wayne Zahn, Atlanta, Ga.	29	212.142
1968—Jim Stefanich, Joliet, Ill.	33	211.895
1969—Billy Hardwick, Louisville, Ky.	33	212.957
1970—Nelson Burton, Jr., St. Louis, Mo.	32	214.908
1971—Don Johnson, Akron, Ohio	31	213.977
1972—Don Johnson, Akron, Ohio	30	215.290
1973—Earl Anthony, Tacoma, Wash.	29	215.799
1974—Earl Anthony, Tacoma, Wash.	27	219.398

STEVE NAGY AWARD

If a husky he-man can be loved by everyone, then Steve Nagy was that man. Nagy, revered by bowlers and bowling, died in 1966 at the too young age of fifty-three. His passing left a big hole in the sport, filled only by the memories of his accomplishments in a lifetime of dedication.

The memory of Steve Nagy has always remained in bowling because he enriched it so much by just being himself to fans and competitors.

As great as Nagy's record was, there was always the lingering question, "Would he have been even greater if he wasn't such a nice guy?"

His fellow pros wanted to remember him as the "nice guy," and the PBA Steve Nagy Sportsmanship Award was established.

Ever since 1966, when the PBA membership first lit a candle in his memory, the tradition goes with an award to the bowler who best fits the mold of Steve Nagy.

The Winners:

1966—John Guenther, Seattle, Wash.

1967—John Guenther, Seattle, Wash.

1968—Ralph Engan, Brookfield, Conn.

1969—Ralph Engan, Brookfield, Conn.

1970—John Guenther, Seattle, Wash.; Dick Ritger, Hartford, Wis.; Dave Soutar, Gilroy, Calif.

1971—Mike Orlovsky, Endicott, N.Y.

1972—Gary Dickinson, Fort Worth, Tex.

1973—Gary Dickinson, Fort Worth, Tex; Dick Ritger, Hartford, Wis.

1974—Gary Dickinson, Fort Worth, Tex.; Alex Seymore, Kannapolis, N.C.

PBA NATIONAL TOURNAMENT CHAMPIONS

WINNER	RUNNERUP
1960—Don Carter, St. Louis, Mo.	Ronnie Gaudern, San Antonio, Tex.
1961—Dave Soutar, Detroit, Mich.	Morrie Oppenheim, Chicago, Ill.
1962—Carmen Salvino, Chicago, Ill.	Don Carter, St. Louis, Mo.
1963—Billy Hardwick, San Mateo, Calif.	Ray Bluth, St. Louis, Mo.
1964—Bob Strampe, Detroit, Mich.	Ray Bluth, St. Louis, Mo.
1965—Dave Davis, Phoenix, Ariz.	Jerry McCoy, Ft. Worth, Tex.
1966—Wayne Zahn, Atlanta, Ga.	Nelson Burton, Jr., St. Louis, Mo.
1967—Dave Davis, Phoenix, Ariz.	Pete Tountas, Tucson, Ariz.
1968—Wayne Zahn, Atlanta, Ga.	Nelson Burton, Jr., St. Louis, Mo.
1969—Mike McGrath, El Cerrito, Calif.	Bill Allen, Fresno, Calif.
1970—Mike McGrath, El Cerrito, Calif.	Dave Davis, Miami, Fla.
1971—Mike Lemongello, N. Babylon, N.Y.	Dave Davis, Miami, Fla.
1972—John Guenther, Seattle, Wash.	Dick Ritger, Hartford, Wis.
1973—Earl Anthony, Tacoma, Wash.	Sam Flanagan, Parkersburg, W. Va.
1974—Earl Anthony, Tacoma, Wash.	Mark Roth, Brooklyn, N.Y.
1975—Earl Anthony, Tacoma, Wash.	Jim Frazier, Spokane, Wash.

ABC MASTERS TOURNAMENT

WINNER	RUNNERUP
1951— Lee Jouglard, Detroit, Mich.	Joe Wilman, Chicago, Ill.
1952—*Willard Taylor, Charleston, W. Va.	Andy Varipapa, Hempstead, N.Y.
1953—*Rudy Habetler, Chicago, Ill.	Ed Brosius, Chicago, Ill.
1954— Eugene Elkins, San Carlos, Calif.	Willard Taylor, Charleston, W. Va.
1955— Buzz Fazio, Detroit, Mich.	Joe Kristof, Chicago, Ill.
1956— Dick Hoover, Akron, Ohio	Ray Bluth, St. Louis, Mo.
1957—*Dick Hoover, Akron, Ohio	Bill Lillard, Dallas, Tex.
1958— Tom Hennessey, St. Louis, Mo.	Lou Frantz, Louisville, Ky.
1959— Ray Bluth, St. Louis, Mo.	Billy Golembiewski, Detroit, Mich.
1960— Bill Golembiewski, Detroit, Mich.	Steve Nagy, St. Louis, Mo.
1961—*Don Carter, St. Louis, Mo.	Dick Hoover, St. Louis, Mo.
1962— Billy Golembiewski, Detroit, Mich.	Ron Winger, Los Angeles, Calif.
1963— Harry Smith, St. Louis, Mo.	Bobby Meadows, Dallas, Tex.
1964— Billy Welu, St. Louis, Mo.	Harry Smith, Baltimore, Md.
1965—*Billy Welu, St. Louis, Mo.	Don Ellis, Houston, Tex.
1966— Bob Strampe, Detroit, Mich.	Al Thompson, Cleveland, Ohio
1967— Lou Scalia, Miami, Fla.	Bill Johnson, New Orleans, La.
1968—*Pete Tountas, Tucson, Ariz.	Buzz Fazio, Detroit, Mich.
1969—*Jim Chestney, Denver, Colo.	Barry Asher, Costa Mesa, Calif.
1970—*Don Glover, Bakersfield, Calif.	Bob Strampe, Detroit, Mich.
1971—*Jim Godman, Lorain, Ohio	Don Johnson, Akron, Ohio
1972—*Bill Beach, Sharon, Pa.	Jim Godman, Lorain, Ohio
1973—Dave Soutar, Kansas City, Mo.	Dick Ritger, Hartford, Wis.
1974—Paul Colwell, Tucson, Ariz.	Steve Neff, Sarasota, Fla.
1975—Ed Ressler, Allentown, Pa.	Sam Flanagan, Parkersburg, W. Va.

*From losers' bracket, won both matches in finals.

BPAA ALL-STAR TOURNAMENT CHAMPIONS
(Renamed U.S. Open in 1971 and made stop on PBA's winter tour.)

WINNER	RUNNERUP
1941-42—John Crimmins, Detroit, Mich.	Joe Norris, Detroit, Mich.
1942-43—Connie Schwoegler, Madison, Wis.	Frank Benkovic, Milwaukee, Wis.
1943-44—Ned Day, Milwaukee, Wis.	Paul Krumske, Chicago, Ill.
1944-45—Buddy Bomar, Chicago, Ill.	Joe Wilman, Berwyn, Ill.
1945-46—Joe Wilman, Chicago, Ill.	Therman Gibson, Detroit, Mich.
1946-47—Andy Varipapa, Hempstead, N.Y.	Allie Brandt, Lockport, N.Y.
1947-48—Andy Varipapa, Hempstead, N.Y.	Joe Wilman, Berwyn, Ill.
1948-49—Connie Schwoegler, Madison, Wis.	Andy Varipapa, Hempstead, N.Y.
1949-50—Junie McMahon, Chicago, Ill.	Ralph Smith, Los Angeles, Calif.
1950-51—Dick Hoover, Akron, Ohio	Lee Jouglard, Detroit, Mich.
1951-52—Junie McMahon, Chicago, Ill.	Bill Lillard, Chicago, Ill.
1952-53—Don Carter, Detroit, Mich.	Ed Lubanski, Detroit, Mich.
1953-54—Don Carter, Detroit, Mich.	Bill Lillard, Chicago, Ill.
1954-55—Steve Nagy, Cleveland, Ohio	Ed Lubanski, Detroit, Mich.
1955-56—Bill Lillard, Chicago, Ill.	Joe Wilman, Chicago, Ill.
1956-57—Don Carter, St. Louis, Mo.	Dick Weber, St. Louis, Mo.
1957-58—Don Carter, St. Louis, Mo.	Buzz Fazio, St. Louis, Mo.
1958-59—Billy Welu, St. Louis, Mo.	Ray Bluth, St. Louis, Mo.
1959-60—Harry Smith, St. Louis, Mo.	Bob Chase, Kansas City, Mo.
1960-61—Bill Tucker, St. Louis, Mo.	Dick Weber, St. Louis, Mo.
1961-62—Dick Weber, St. Louis, Mo. (new format)	Roy Lown, El Paso, Tex.
1962-63—Dick Weber, St. Louis, Mo. (new format)	Billy Welu, St. Louis, Mo.
1963-64—Bob Strampe, Detroit, Mich. (new format)	Tommy Tuttle, Rural Hall, N.C.
1964-65—Dick Weber, St. Louis, Mo. (new format)	Jim St. John, Santa Clara, Calif.
1965-66—Dick Weber, St. Louis, Mo. (new format)	Nelson Burton, Jr., St. Louis, Mo.
1966-67—Les Schissler, Denver, Colo. (new format)	Pete Tountas, Tucson, Ariz.
1967-68—Jim Stefanich, Joliet, Ill.	Billy Hardwick, San Mateo, Calif.
1968-69—Billy Hardwick, Louisville, Ky.	Dick Weber, St. Louis, Mo.
1969-70—Bobby Cooper, Houston, Tex.	Billy Hardwick, Louisville, Ky.
1971 —Mike Lemongello, N. Babylon, N.Y.	Teata Semiz, River Edge, N.J.
1972 —Don Johnson, Akron, Ohio	George Pappas, Charlotte, N.C.
1973—Mike McGrath, St. Louis, Mo.	Earl Anthony, Tacoma, Wash.
1974—Larry Laub, San Francisco	Dave Davis, Atlanta, Ga.
1975—Steve Neff, Sarasota, Fla.	Paul Colwell, Tucson, Ariz.

WORLD'S INVITATIONAL CHAMPIONS

WINNER	RUNNERUP
1957—Don Carter, St. Louis, Mo.	Tom Hennessey, St. Louis, Mo.
1958—Ed Lubanski, Detroit, Mich.	Don Carter, St. Louis, Mo.
1959—Don Carter, St. Louis, Mo.	Bill Golembiewski, Detroit, Mich.
1960—Don Carter, St. Louis, Mo.	Joe Joseph, Detroit, Mich.
1961—Don Carter, St. Louis, Mo.	Ray Bluth, St. Louis, Mo.
1962—Don Carter, St. Louis, Mo.	Ray Bluth, St. Louis, Mo.
1963—Jim St. John, San Jose, Calif.	John Meyer, Lake Ronkonkoma, N.Y.
1964—Jim St. John, San Jose, Calif.	Bob Strampe, Detroit, Mich.

(Tournament suspended after 1964)

PBA CHAMPIONS SINCE THE BEGINNING

1959 Tournaments

	PURSE	WINNER	1ST PLACE MONEY
Empire State, Albany, N.Y.	$ 16,500	Lou Campi, Dumont, N.J.	$ 2,500
Paramus-Eastern, Paramus, N.J.	17,000	Dick Weber, St. Louis, Mo.	2,500
Dayton Open, Dayton, Ohio	16,000	Dick Weber, St. Louis, Mo.	2,600

1960 Tournaments

	PURSE	WINNER	1ST PLACE MONEY
Empire State, Albany, N.Y.	$ 16,500	Dick Weber, St. Louis, Mo.	$ 2,500
Fairless Hills (Pa.) Open	15,300	Bill Bunetta, Fresno, Cal.	2,500
Paramus-Eastern, Paramus, N.J.	17,400	Don Carter, St. Louis, Mo.	3,000
Showboat Inv't'l, Las Vegas, Nev.	21,900	Tom Hennessey, St. Louis, Mo.	3,500
No. Calif. (San Francisco) Open	18,100	Earl Johnson, Minneapolis, Minn.	2,500
So. Calif. (Los Angeles) Open	22,600	Morrie Oppenheim, Chicago, Ill.	3,000

1961 Tournaments

	PURSE	WINNER	1ST PLACE MONEY
Empire State, Albany, N.Y.	$ 17,000	Carmen Salvino, Chicago, Ill.	$ 3,000
Nat'l Inv't'l, Paramus, N.J.	75,000	Roy Lown, Baltimore, Md.	15,000
All-American, Dallas, Tex.	21,900	Dick Weber, St. Louis, Mo.	3,000

	PURSE	WINNER	1ST PLACE MONEY
Shreveport (La.) Open	$ 10,000	Dick Weber, St. Louis, Mo.	$ 1,500
Fred Magee Open, Houston, Tex.	25,000	Dick Weber, St. Louis, Mo.	3,000
El Paso (Texas) Open	19,400	Harry Smith, St. Louis, Mo.	2,500
West. Reg., Redondo Beach, Cal.	21,900	Dick Weber, St. Louis, Mo.	3,000
San Jose (Calif.) Open	21,900	Dick Weber, St. Louis, Mo.	3,000
No. Calif., Open, San Francisco	19,400	Vern Downing, Rodeo, Calif.	2,500
Showboat Inv't'l, Las Vegas, Nev.	26,900	George Howard, Detroit, Mich.	4,000

1962 Tournaments

	PURSE	WINNER	1ST PLACE MONEY
Benesch Open, Argo, Ill.	$ 20,000	Dick Weber, St. Louis, Mo.	$ 4,000
Puerto Rico Inv't'l	10,000	Dick Weber, St. Louis, Mo.	4,000
Empire State, Albany, N.Y.	25,000	Fred Lening, Fairless Hills, Pa.	5,000
Philadelphia (Pa.) Open	23,900	Harry Smith, Baltimore, Md.	5,000
Colt Open, Baltimore, Md.	25,200	Dick Hoover, Akron, Ohio	5,000
Coca Cola Open, Akron, Ohio	25,200	Glen Blakesley, Kansas City, Mo.	5,000
Coca Cola Open, Cleveland, Ohio	25,200	Skip Vigars, Albany, N.Y.	5,000
Winston-Salem (N.C.) Open	22,800	Al Savas, Milwaukee, Wis.	5,000
Birmingham (Ala.) Open	23,900	Andy Rogoznica, Chicago, Ill.	5,000
Memphis (Tenn.) Open	25,200	Glenn Allison, St. Louis, Mo.	5,000
Houston (Tex.) Open	25,200	Don Carter, St. Louis, Mo.	5,075
Oak Hills Open, San Antonio, Tex.	25,200	Don Bickford, Oakland, Calif.	5,000
Coca Cola Open, Okla. City	22,800	Tom Hennessey, St. Louis, Mo.	5,000
Coca Cola Open, St. Louis, Mo.	25,200	Joe Joseph, Lansing, Mich.	5,000

(continued on next page)

	PURSE	WINNER	1ST PLACE MONEY
San Jose (Calif.) Open	$ 25,200	J. B. Solomon, Dallas, Tex.	$ 5,000
Showboat Inv't'l, Las Vegas, Nev.	36,200	Dick Agee, San Jose, Calif.	6,000
Indianapolis (Ind.) Open	30,000	Billy Welu, St. Louis, Mo.	4,000
Tour of Champs, Indianapolis	50,000	Joe Joseph, Lansing, Mich.	15,000
Canadian Open, Montreal, Can.	30,000	Tom Hennessey, St. Louis, Mo.	4,000
Santa Fair Open, Seattle, Wash.	20,200	Don Carter, St. Louis, Mo.	3,000
Silver Lanes Open, Spokane, Wash.	20,200	Darylee Cox, Seattle, Wash.	3,000
Salt Lake City (Utah) Open	17,000	Glenn Allison, St. Louis, Mo.	2,500
So. Calif.(Long Beach) Open	20,000	Al Savas, Milwaukee, Wis.	2,800
Tucson (Arizona) Open	20,200	Don Carter, St. Louis, Mo.	2,800
All-American, Dallas, Tex.	20,000	Ray Orf, St. Louis, Mo.	2,750
Twin City (St. Paul, Minn.) Open	20,300	Andy Marzich, Long Beach, Calif.	3,000
Chicago (Ill.) Open	23,400	Ed Lubanski, Detroit, Mich.	3,000
Pontiac (Mich.) Open	23,400	Carmen Salvino, Chicago, Ill.	3,000
Niagara Falls (N.Y.) Open	23,400	George Howard, Detroit, Mich.	3,000
Labor Day Classic, Latham, N.Y.	20,800	Dick Downey, Bloomfield, N.J.	2,700
Rochester (N.Y.) Open	23,400	Don Carter, St. Louis, Mo.	3,200

1963 Tournaments

	PURSE	WINNER	1ST PLACE MONEY
Coca Cola Open, Atlanta, Ga.	$ 23,500	Dennis Chapis, St. Louis, Mo.	$ 5,000
Charlotte (N.C.) Open	20,000	Billy Golembiewski, Detroit, Mich.	4,000
Coca Cola Open, Denver, Colo.	23,500	Andy Marzich, Long Beach, Calif.	5,050
Coca Cola Open, Louisville, Ky.	23,500	Earl Johnson, Minneapolis, Minn.	5,000

	PURSE	WINNER	1ST PLACE MONEY
Coca Cola Open, St. Louis, Mo.	$ 23,500	Andy Marzich, Long Beach, Calif.	$ 5,050
Coca Cola "Stars," Mid. City, Okla.	23,500	Glenn Allison, St. Louis, Mo.	5,000
All American Classic, Dallas, Tex.	23,500	A. W. "Bill" Johnson, St. Louis, Mo.	5,000
Houston (Tex.) Charity Classic	20,500	Johnny Meyer, Neconset, N.Y.	4,000
Mobile (Ala.) Sertoma Open	23,500	Billy Hardwick, San Mateo, Calif.	5,000
Coca Cola Open, Gretna, La.	23,500	J. B. Solomon, Dallas, Tex.	5,000
Coca Cola Open, Birmingham, Ala.	23,500	Jack Biondolillo, Houston, Tex.	5,050
Tenn. Open, Kingsport, Tenn.	23,500	Roger Helle, Detroit, Mich.	5,000
Indianapolis (Ind.) 500	26,000	Les Schissler, Denver, Colo.	5,000
Pontiac (Mich.) Open	26,000	Bill Allen, Orlando, Fla.	5,000
Coca Cola Open, Akron, Ohio	25,000	Harry Smith, Baltimore, Md.	5,000
Boston Open, Woburn, Mass.	26,000	Andy Marzich, Long Beach, Cal.	5,000
N.J. Open, N. Brunswick, N.J.	26,000	Dick Weber, St. Louis, Mo.	5,000
Baltimore (Md.) Open	20,400	Lewis Ray, Ft. Worth, Tex.	3,000
Coca Cola Open, Warren, Ohio	23,600	Marty Piraino, Syracuse, N.Y.	3,000
Empire State, Albany, N.Y.	21,000	Earl Johnson, Minneapolis, Minn.	2,500
Canadian Open, Montreal, Can.	20,400	Harry Smith, Baltimore, Md.	3,000
Coca Cola Open, Chicago, Ill.	22,800	Wayne Zahn, Atlanta, Ga.	3,000
Coca Cola Open, Rockford, Ill.	22,000	Jim St. John, San Jose, Calif.	3,000
Alton (Ill.) Open	20,400	Vern Downing, Rodeo, Calif.	3,000
Ft. Smith (Ark.) Open	18,000	Jim St. John, San Jose, Calif.	2,500
Meridian (Miss.) Open	22,000	Jim St. John, San Jose, Calif.	3,000
San Antonio (Tex.) Open	20,400	Bill Allen, Orlando, Fla.	3,000
Tucson (Ariz.) Open	20,400	Jack Biondolillo, Houston, Tex.	3,000
Phoenix Open, Mesa, Ariz.	20,400	Billy Hardwick, San Mateo, Calif.	3,000

(continued on next page)

	PURSE	WINNER	1ST PLACE MONEY
San Diego (Calif.) Open	$ 23,600	Earl Johnson, Minneapolis, Minn.	$ 3,000
L.A. Open, Gardena, Calif.	20,000	Billy Hardwick, San Mateo, Calif.	2,500
San Jose (Calif.) Open	23,600	George Howard, Detroit, Mich.	3,000
Portland (Ore.) Open	20,400	Darylee Cox, Seattle, Wash.	3,000
Coca Cola Open, Seattle, Wash.	20,400	Norm Meyers, Los Angeles, Calif.	3,000
Spokane (Wash.) Open	20,400	Harry Smith, Baltimore, Md.	3,000
Salt Lake City (Utah) Open	20,400	Bill Allen, Orlando, Fla.	2,500
Las Vegas (Nev.) Open	25,000	Dick Weber, St. Louis, Mo.	3,000

1964 Tournaments

	PURSE	WINNER	1ST PLACE MONEY
Jacksonville (Fla.) Open	$ 26,000	Carmen Salvino, Chicago, Ill.	$ 4,000
Hialeah (Fla.) Open	26,000	Johnny King, Chicago, Ill.	4,000
St. Louis (Mo.) Open	25,000	Andy Marzich, Long Beach, Calif.	4,000
Mobile (Ala.) Sertoma Open	25,000	Bill Allen, Orlando, Fla.	4,000
Coca Cola Open, Gretna, La.	27,000	Bill Allen, Orlando, Fla.	4,000
Coca Cola Open, Birmingham, Ala.	25,000	Billy Hardwick, San Mateo, Calif.	4,000
Colt Open, Glen Burnie, Md.	31,000	Tommy Tuttle, King, N.C.	4,000
N.J. Cavalcade, Princeton, N.J.	31,000	Buzz Fazio, Detroit, Mich.	4,000
Buffalo Open, Depew, N.Y.	25,000	Wayne Zahn, Atlanta, Ga.	4,000
No. Amer. Van Lines, Pontiac, Mich.	31,000	Billy Hardwick, San Mateo, Calif.	4,000
Denver (Colo.) Open	25,000	Don Johnson, Kokomo, Ind.	4,000
So. Calif. Open, Costa Mesa, Calif.	27,500	Billy Hardwick, San Mateo, Calif.	4,000
No. Calif. Open, Lodi, Calif.	25,000	Wayne Zahn, Atlanta, Ga.	4,000

	PURSE	WINNER	1ST PLACE MONEY
San Jose (Calif.) Open	$ 30,000	Bill Allen, Orlando, Fla.	$ 4,000
Coca Cola Open, Seattle, Wash.	21,000	Jerry McCoy, Ft. Worth, Tex.	3,000
Spokane (Wash.) Open	21,400	Ray Bluth, St. Louis, Mo.	3,000
Coca Cola Open, Rockford, Ill.	24,500	Carmen Salvino, Chicago, Ill.	3,000
Pittsburgh Open, Baden, Pa.	21,000	Harry Smith, Baltimore, Md.	3,000
Continental Open, Detroit, Mich.	27,500	Jim St. John, San Jose, Calif.	3,000
Canadian Open, Montreal, Can.	24,500	Bill Allen, Orlando, Fla.	3,000
Bertrand Open, Waukegan, Ill.	27,500	Pete Tountas, Hammond, Ind.	3,000
Coca Cola Open, Louisville, Ky.	24,500	Nelson Burton, Jr., St. Louis, Mo.	3,000
Coca Cola Open, Houston, Tex.	21,000	Les Schissler, Denver, Colo.	3,000
Hart Furniture Open, Dallas, Tex.	21,000	Dick Weber, St. Louis, Mo.	3,000
Tucson (Ariz.) Open	21,000	Glenn Allison, Los Angeles, Calif.	3,000
Mesa-Phoenix (Ariz.) Open	21,500	Billy Welu, St. Louis, Mo.	3,000
San Diego (Calif.) Open	24,500	Andy Marzich, Los Angeles, Calif.	3,000
Oxnard (Calif.) Open	24,500	Glenn Allison, Los Angeles, Calif.	3,000
Las Vegas (Nev.) Open	30,000	Harry Smith, Boston, Mass.	4,000
Pepsi Cola Open, Columbus, Ohio	27,500	Billy Golembiewski, Detroit, Mich.	3,000

1965 Tournaments

	PURSE	WINNER	1ST PLACE MONEY
No. Calif. Open, Sacramento, Calif.	$ 28,500	Buzz Fazio, Detroit, Mich.	$ 5,000
So. Calif. Open, Costa Mesa, Calif.	28,500	Jerry Hale, Richmond, Calif.	5,000
Hialeah-Miami (Fla.) Open	28,500	Billy Golembiewski, Detroit, Mich.	5,000
Mobile (Ala.) Sertoma Open	30,000	Billy Golembiewski, Detroit, Mich.	5,000

(continued on next page)

	PURSE	WINNER	1ST PLACE MONEY
Parkersburg (W. Va.) Open	$ 31,000	Fred Lening, Fairless Hills, Pa.	$ 5,000
Thunderbird Open, Wichita, Kan.	28,500	Dick Weber, St. Louis, Mo.	5,000
Pike's Peak Open, Colo. Spgs., Colo.	28,500	Dave Soutar, Detroit, Mich.	5,000
Oklahoma City (Okla.) Open	28,500	Mike Lemongello, N. Babylon, N.Y.	5,000
Madison (Wis.) Open	28,500	Earl Johnson, Minneapolis, Minn.	5,000
Continental Open, Detroit, Mich.	34,000	Bob Strampe, Detroit, Mich.	5,000
Fairlanes Open, Depew, N.Y.	32,000	Bill Allen, Orlando, Fla.	5,000
Ins. City Classic, Hart., Conn.	34,500	Bill Allen, Orlando, Fla.	5,000
Firestone Tour. of Champs, Akron, Ohio	100,000	Billy Hardwick, San Mateo, Calif.	25,000
Venezuela Open, Caracas, Venez.	20,000	Harry Smith, Redwood City, Calif.	2,000
Seattle (Wash.) Open	22,500	Gene Rhoda, Valparaiso, Ind.	3,000
Portland (Ore.) Open	22,500	Mike McGrath, El Cerrito, Calif.	3,000
San Jose (Calif.) Open	30,000	Bill Tucker, Los Angeles, Calif.	4,000
Tucson (Ariz.) Squirt Open	22,500	Harry Smith, Redwood City, Calif.	3,000
Salt Lake City (Utah) Open	22,500	Dave Davis, Phoenix, Ariz.	3,000
Denver (Colo.) Open	22,500	Harry Smith, Redwood City, Calif.	3,000
Louisville (Ky.) Open	25,500	Gene Rhoda, Valparaiso, Ind.	3,000
Boston Open, Brockton, Mass.	28,500	Johnny Meyer, L. Ronkonkoma, N.Y.	3,000
Bergen Mall Open, Paramus, N.J.	27,000	Carmen Salvino, Chicago, Ill.	3,000
Bertrand Open, Waukegan, Ill.	28,500	Tom Harnisch, Buffalo, N.Y.	3,000
Labor Day Classic, Dallas, Tex.	24,000	Sam Baca, Union City, Calif.	3,000
Birmingham (Ala.) Open	22,500	Carmen Salvino, Chicago, Ill.	3,000
Nashville (Tenn.) Kiwanis Open	22,500	Gary Martineau, Nashville, Tenn.	3,000
Houston (Tex.) Open	22,500	Dick Weber, St. Louis, Mo.	2,500

	PURSE	WINNER	1ST PLACE MONEY
No. Calif. Open, S. Francisco	$ 22,500	Bob Strampe, Detroit, Mich.	$ 3,000
Oxnard (Calif.) Open	22,500	Johnny Guenther, Seattle, Wash.	3,000
Las Vegas (Nev.) Open	30,000	Bob Collatos, Santa Monica, Calif.	4,000

1966 Tournaments

Eastern Open, Edison, N.J.	$ 35,000	Dennis Chapis, St. Louis, Mo.	$ 5,000
Charlotte (N.C.) Open	35,000	Gene Rhoda, Valparaiso, Ind.	5,000
Western Open, San Jose, Calif.	30,000	Jim Godman, Hayward, Calif.	5,000
Denver (Colo.) Open	35,000	Dick Weber, St. Louis, Mo.	5,000
Hialeah-Miami (Fla.) Open	35,000	Les Schissler, Denver, Colo.	5,000
Mobile (Ala.) Sertoma Open	35,000	Mike Lemongello, N. Babylon, N.Y.	5,000
Fresno (Calif.) Open	35,000	Dick Weber, St. Louis, Mo.	5,000
Showboat Inv't'l, Las Vegas, Nev.	40,000	Skee Foremsky, El Paso, Tex.	7,500
Miller Open, Milwaukee, Wis.	60,000	Bill Lillard, Dallas, Tex.	10,000
St. Paul (Minn.) Open	37,000	Gene Rhoda, Valparaiso, Ind.	5,000
Buckeye Open, Toledo, Ohio	38,500	Pete Tountas, Tucson, Ariz.	5,000
Buffalo Open, Depew, N.Y.	37,000	Bobby Jacks, New Orleans, La.	5,000
Firestone Tour. of Champs, Akron, Ohio	100,000	Wayne Zahn, Atlanta, Ga.	25,000
Seattle (Wash. Open	27,500	Wayne Zahn, Atlanta, Ga.	3,000
Portland (Ore.) Open	27,500	Don Johnson, Kokomo, Ind.	3,000
Fresno (Calif.) Open	29,000	Les Schissler, Denver, Colo.	3,000
Tucson (Ariz.) Squirt Open	27,500	Johnny Guenther, Seattle, Wash.	3,000
So. Calif. Open, Encino, Calif.	29,000	Barry Asher, Santa Monica, Calif.	3,000
Ft. Worth (Tex.) Open	27,500	Dick Ritger, Hartford, Wis.	3,000
Reading (Pa.) Open	27,500	Dick Ritger, Hartford, Wis.	3,000

(continued on next page)

PBA CHAMPIONS SINCE THE BEGINNING (cont.)

	PURSE	WINNER	1ST PLACE MONEY
Coast Guard Open, G. Haven, Mich.	$ 30,000	George Howard, Detroit, Mich.	$ 3,000
Brockton (Mass.) Open	34,000	Bobby Jacks, New Orleans, La.	3,000
Waukegan (Ill.) Open	34,000	Bobby Jacks, New Orleans, La.	3,000
Ft. Smith (Ark.) Open	27,500	John Petraglia, Brooklyn, N.Y.	3,000
Labor Day Classic, Dallas, Tex.	27,500	Bud Horn, Los Angeles, Calif.	3,000
Crescent City Open, New Orleans, La.	27,500	Barry Asher, Santa Ana, Calif.	3,000
Camden (N.J.) Open	31,000	Ralph Engan, Monsey, N.Y.	3,000
Baltimore (Md.) Open	34,000	Jim Stefanich, Chicago, Ill.	3,000

1967 Tournaments

	PURSE	WINNER	1ST PLACE MONEY
Tucson (Ariz.) Open	$ 40,000	John Juni, Hollywood, Fla.	$ 5,000
Western Open, San Jose, Calif.	40,000	Jim St. John, San Jose, Calif.	5,000
Showboat Inv't'l, Las Vegas, Nev.	50,000	Dave Davis, Phoenix, Ariz.	10,000
Denver (Colo.) Open	35,000	Dave Davis, Phoenix, Ariz.	5,000
St. Paul (Minn.) Open	50,000	Carmen Salvino, Chicago, Ill.	10,000
Brut Open, Kansas City, Mo.	50,000	Tim Harahan, Encino, Calif.	10,000
Buckeye Open, Toledo, Ohio	40,000	Jim St. John, San Jose, Calif.	5,000
Miller Open, Milwaukee, Wis.	60,000	Dave Davis, Phoenix, Ariz.	10,000
Ebonite Open, Edison, N.J.	50,000	Sam Baca, Hayward, Calif.	7,500
Buffalo Open, Depew, N.Y.	37,000	Nelson Burton, Jr., St. Louis, Mo.	5,000
Tampa (Fla.) Sertoma Open	40,000	Mike Durbin, Costa Mesa, Calif.	5,000
Mobile (Ala.) Sertoma Open	40,000	Carmen Salvino, Chicago, Ill.	5,000
Firestone Tour. of Champs, Akron, Ohio	100,000	Jim Stefanich, Joliet, Ill.	25,000

	PURSE	WINNER	1ST PLACE MONEY
Seattle (Wash.) Open	$ 27,500	Don Johnson, Kokomo, Ind.	$ 3,000
Portland (Ore.) Open	27,500	Les Schissler, Denver, Colo.	3,000
Fresno (Calif.) Open	27,500	Dick Ritger, Hartford, Wis.	3,000
El Paso (Tex.) Optimists Club Open	27,500	Bill Tucker, Los Angeles, Calif.	3,000
Houston (Tex.) Sertoma Open	27,500	Butch Gearhart, Ft. Lauderdale, Fla.	3,000
Ft. Worth (Tex.) Open	27,500	Dave Soutar, Detroit, Mich.	3,000
Oklahoma City (Okla.) Open	27,500	Butch Gearhart, Ft. Lauderdale, Fla.	3,000
Ft. Smith (Ark.) Open	27,500	Jim Stefanich, Joliet, Ill.	3,000
Brockton (Mass.) Open	30,500	Don Johnson, Kokomo, Ind.	3,000
Coast Guard Open, G. Haven, Mich.	30,000	Jim Stefanich, Joliet, Ill.	3,000
Waukegan (Ill.) Open	34,000	Jim Godman, Hayward, Calif.	3,000
Green Bay (Wis.) Open	27,500	Dave Davis, Phoenix, Ariz.	3,000
Neb. Cent. Open, Omaha, Neb.	30,500	Dave Davis, Phoenix, Ariz.	3,000
Lubbock (Tex.) Open	27,500	Skee Foremsky, El Paso, Tex.	3,000
Lions Club Open, New Orleans, La.	27,500	Bill Tucker, Los Angeles, Calif.	3,000
Kokomo (Ind.) Open	27,500	Billy Hardwick, San Mateo, Calif.	3,000
Youngstown (Ohio) Open	30,500	Mike Durbin, Costa Mesa, Calif.	3,000
Plainville (Conn.) Open	30,500	Don Helling, St. Louis, Mo.	3,000
Durham (N.C.) Open	27,500	Wayne Zahn, Atlanta, Ga.	3,000
Camden (N.J.) Open	30,500	George Howard, Kalamazoo, Mich.	3,000

1968 Tournaments

	PURSE	WINNER	1ST PLACE MONEY
Phoenix (Ariz.) Open	$ 40,000	Dick Ritger, Hartford, Wis.	$ 6,000
Showboat Inv't'l, Las Vegas, Nev.	55,000	Bill Allen, Orlando, Fla.	10,000

(continued on next page)

PBA CHAMPIONS SINCE THE BEGINNING (cont.)

	PURSE	WINNER	1ST PLACE MONEY
San Jose (Calif.) Open	$ 50,000	Bill Allen, Orlando, Fla.	$ 7,000
Denver (Colo.) Open	40,000	Dave Soutar, Detroit, Mich.	6,000
Cougar Open, Kansas City, Mo.	25,000	Mike Lemongello, Seattle, Wash.	10,000
Tampa (Fla.) Sertoma Open	40,000	Jim Stefanich, Joliet, Ill.	6,000
Buckeye Open, Toledo, Ohio	45,000	Jim Stefanich, Joliet, Ill.	6,000
Miller Open, Milwaukee, Wis.	60,000	Johnny Guenther, Seattle, Wash.	10,000
Buffalo Open, Depew, N.Y.	45,000	Bob Strampe, Detroit, Mich.	6,000
Ebonite Gold Cup, M'tainside, N.J.	60,000	Teata Semiz, River Edge, N.J.	8,000
Lions Open, New Orleans, La.	40,000	Dick Ritger, Hartford, Wis.	6,000
Firestone Tour. of Champs, Akron, Ohio	100,000	Dave Davis, Phoenix, Ariz.	25,000
Ebonite Inv't'l, St. Louis, Mo.	15,000	Don Glover, Bakersfield, Calif.	2,000
Mobile (Ala.) Sertoma Open	40,000	Jim Stefanich, Joliet, Ill.	6,000
Seattle (Wash.) Open	30,000	Billy Hardwick, Louisville, Ky.	3,000
Portland (Ore.). Open	30,000	Jim Stefanich, Joliet, Ill.	3,000
Fresno (Calif.) Open	32,000	Jim Stefanich, Joliet, Ill.	3,000
Tucson (Ariz.) Open	30,000	Tim Harahan, Encino, Calif.	3,000
El Paso (Tex.) Open	30,000	Mike Durbin, Burbank, Calif.	3,000
Ft. Worth (Tex.) Open	30,000	Don McCune, Munster, Ind.	3,000
Houston (Tex.) Sertoma Open	30,000	Wayne Zahn, Atlanta, Ga.	3,000
Coast Guard Open, G. Haven, Mich.	30,000	Bill Allen, Orlando, Fla.	3,000
Waukegan (Ill.) Open	30,000	Bob Strampe, Detroit, Mich.	3,000
Canadian Open, Montreal, Can.	30,000	Skee Foremsky, El Paso, Tex.	3,000
Rochester (N.Y.) Open	30,000	Tim Harahan, Encino, Calif.	3,000
Portsmouth-Norfolk (Va.) Open	30,000	Don Johnson, Kokomo, Ind.	3,000

	PURSE	WINNER	1ST PLACE MONEY
Altoona (Pa.) Open	$ 30,000	Jim Godman, Hayward, Ind.	$ 3,000
Newark (Ohio) Open	30,000	Bill Allen, Orlando, Fla.	3,000
Mercury Open, Edison, N.J.	40,000	Wayne Zahn, Atlanta, Ga.	3,000
Japan Gold Cup, Tokyo, Japan	20,000	Don Johnson, Kokomo, Ind.	2,000
Green Bay (Wis.) Open	30,000	Mike McGrath, El Cerrito, Calif.	3,000
Joliet (Ill.) Open	30,000	Don Glover, Bakersfield, Calif.	3,000
Durham (N.C.) Open	30,000	Dave Davis, Phoenix, Ariz.	3,000

1969 Tournaments

	PURSE	WINNER	1ST PLACE MONEY
West Valley (L.A.) Open	$ 45,000	Wayne Zahn, Atlanta, Ga.	$ 6,000
Valley of Sun Open, Tempe, Ariz.	45,000	Don Glover, Bakersfield, Calif.	6,000
Showboat Inv't'l, Las Vegas, Nev.	60,000	Skee Foremsky, El Paso, Tex.	10,000
San Jose (Calif.) Open	60,000	Johnny Guenther, Fresno, Calif.	6,000
Denver (Colo.) Open	45,000	Billy Hardwick, Louisville, Ky.	6,000
Ebonite Open, Kansas City, Mo.	60,000	Don Glover, Bakersfield, Calif.	8,000
Cougar Open, Paramus, N.J.	75,000	Ralph Engan, Monsey, N.Y.	10,000
Buffalo Open, Depew, N.Y.	45,000	Dick Ritger, Hartford, Wis.	6,000
Miller Open, Milwaukee, Wis.	70,000	Billy Hardwick, Louisville, Ky.	10,000
Buckeye Open, Toledo, Ohio	50,000	Ray Bluth, St. Louis, Mo.	6,000
Portsmouth (Va.) Open	45,000	Tommy Tuttle, King, N.C.	6,000
New Orleans Lions Open, New Orleans, La.	45,000	Dick Weber, St. Louis, Mo.	6,000
Firestone Tour. of Champs, Akron, Ohio	100,000	Jim Godman, Hayward, Calif.	25,000
Pro-Am Classic, Mobile, Ala.	12,300	Don Helling, St. Louis, Mo.	1,200

(continued on next page)

	PURSE	WINNER	1ST PLACE MONEY
Smallcomb Classic, Redwood City, Calif.	$ 60,000	Billy Hardwick, Louisville, Ky.	$ 6,000
Seattle (Wash.) Open	32,000	Don Johnson, Kokomo, Ind.	3,000
Portland (Ore.) Open	32,000	Allie Clarke, Akron, Ohio	3,000
Tucson (Ariz.) Open	32,000	Terry Booth, Mount. View, Calif.	3,000
Ft. Worth (Tex.) Open	32,000	Billy Hardwick, Louisville, Ky.	3,000
Houston (Tex.) Sertoma Open	32,000	Marty Piraino, Syracuse, N.Y.	3,000
Huntsville (Ala.) Open	32,000	Joe Dignam, Edmonds, Wash.	3,000
Five Star Open, Cranston, R.I.	35,000	Nelson Burton, Jr., St. Louis, Mo.	3,000
Grand Rapids (Mich.) Open	32,000	Billy Hardwick, Louisville, Ky.	3,000
Waukegan (Ill.) Open	38,000	Les Zikes, Chicago, Ill.	3,000
Canadian Open, Montreal, Can.	35,000	Dave Davis, Phoenix, Ariz.	3,000
Altoona (Pa.) Jaycee Open	32,000	Dick Weber, St. Louis, Mo.	3,000
Newark (O.) Kiwanis Open	32,000	Butch Gearhart, Ft. Lauderdale, Fla.	3,000
Japan Gold Cup, Tokyo, Japan	20,000	Dick Ritger, Hartford, Wis.	2,000
Mercury Open, St. Louis, Mo.	40,000	Jim Godman, Elkhart, Ind.	4,000
Amer. Airlines Open, Detroit, Mich.	50,000	Dave Soutar, Gilroy, Calif.	6,000
Joliet (Ill.) Open	32,000	Billy Hardwick, Louisville, Ky.	3,000
Lincoln (Neb.) Open	32,000	Don Johnson, Kokomo, Ind.	3,000
Bellows-Valvair Open, Roch., N.Y.	50,000	Dick Ritger, Hartford, Wis.	6,000
Hawaiian Inv't'l, Honolulu	12,500	Don Johnson, Kokomo, Ind.	2,000

1970 Tournaments

	PURSE	WINNER	1ST PLACE MONEY
Wichita (Kan.) Open	$ 45,000	Skee Foremsky, Houston, Texas	$ 6,000
Greater Los Angeles Open	50,000	Ed Bourdase, Fresno, Calif.	6,000

	PURSE	WINNER	1ST PLACE MONEY
Showboat Inv't'l, Las Vegas, Nev.	$ 77,777	Dave Soutar, Gilroy, Calif.	$11,111
San Jose (Calif.) Open	65,000	Dave Davis, Miami, Fla.	10,000
Denver (Colo.) Open	45,000	Nelson Burton, Jr., St. Louis, Mo.	6,000
Ebonite Open, Kansas City, Mo.	60,000	Jim Stefanich, Joliet, Ill.	8,000
Miller Open, Milwaukee, Wis.	70,000	George Pappas, Charlotte, N.C.	10,000
Buckeye Open, Toledo, Ohio	50,000	Nelson Burton, Jr., St. Louis, Mo.	6,000
Don Carter Classic, N.Y.C.	60,000	Mike Lemongello, N. Babylon, N.Y.	7,500
Buffalo Open, Depew, N.Y.	45,000	George Pappas, Charlotte, N.C.	6,000
Cougar Open, Miami, Fla.	75,000	Mike McGrath, El Cerrito, Calif.	10,000
New Orleans (La.) Lions Open	45,000	Don Johnson, Akron, Ohio	6,000
Firestone Tour. of Champs, Akron, Ohio	100,000	Wayne Zahn, Tempe, Ariz.	2,000
Pro-Am Classic (Atlanta)	20,000	Earl Anthony, Tacoma, Wash.	3,000
Seattle (Wash.) Open	32,000	Don Glover, Bakersfield, Calif.	3,000
Portland (Oregon) Open	32,500	Mike Durbin, Dayton, Ohio	6,000
Bellows-Valvair Open, Redwood City, Calif.	50,000	Marty Piraino, Syracuse, N.Y.	3,000
Fresno (Calif.) Open	32,000	Larry Laub, San Francisco, Calif.	3,000
Tucson (Arizona) Open	32,000	Nelson Burton, Jr., St. Louis, Mo.	3,000
El Paso (Texas) Open	30,000	Don McCune, Munster, Ind.	3,000
Sertoma Open, Houston, Tex.	34,000	Nelson Burton, Jr., St. Louis, Mo.	3,000
Ft. Worth (Tex.) Open	30,000	Dick Battista, Astoria, N.Y.	3,000
Grand Rapids (Mich.) Open	37,000	Dave Soutar, Gilroy, Calif.	3,000
Waukegan (Ill.) Open	38,000	Jim Stefanich, Joliet, Ill.	4,000
Gansett Open, Cranston, R.I.	40,000	Johnny Petraglia, Brooklyn, N.Y.	5,000
Bellows-Valvair Open, Pittsburgh, Pa.	50,000	Curt Schmidt, Ft. Wayne, Ind.	3,000
Blue Mt. Open, Windgap, Pa.	32,000	Dick Ritger, Hartford, Wis.	2,000

(continued on next page)

PBA CHAMPIONS SINCE THE BEGINNING (cont.)

	PURSE	WINNER	1ST PLACE MONEY
Japan Gold Cup, Tokyo, Japan	$ 20,000	Dave Soutar, Gilroy, Calif.	$ 5,000
PBA National Champ., Garden City, N.Y.	70,000	Dave Soutar, Gilroy, Calif.	3,000
Bellows-Valvair Open, St. Louis, Mo.	50,000	Bud Horn, Los Angeles, Calif.	New Car
Lincoln (Neb.) Open	32,000	Dave Soutar, Gilroy, Calif.	6,000
Mercury Open, Okla. City, Okla.	40,000	Teata Semiz, River Edge, N.J.	6,000
American Airlines Open, Detroit, Mich.	50,000	Dick Weber, St. Louis, Mo.	2,000
Bellows-Valvair Open, Rochester, N.Y.	50,000	Don Johnson, Akron, Ohio	25,000
Hawaiian Inv't'l, Honolulu	12,000	Mike McGrath, El Cerrito, Calif.	7,500

1971 Tournaments

	PURSE	WINNER	1ST PLACE MONEY
BPAA U.S. Open, St. Paul, Minn.	$ 75,000	Mike Lemongello, N. Babylon, N.Y.	$ 8,000
Denver (Colo.) Open	50,000	Dick Weber, St. Louis, Mo.	6,000
Showboat Inv't'l, Las Vegas, Nev.	77,777	Don Johnson, Akron, Ohio	11,111
Los Angeles (Calif.) Open	50,000	Dave Soutar, Gilroy, Calif.	6,000
Ebonite Open, San Jose, Calif.	75,000	Larry Lichstein, Windsor Locks, Conn.	10,000
STP Classic, Kansas City, Mo.	70,000	Johnny Guenther, Fresno, Calif.	10,000
Winston-Salem (N.C.) Classic	80,000	Johnny Petraglia, Brooklyn, N.Y.	10,000
Miller Open, Milwaukee, Wis.	70,000	Dave Soutar, Gilroy, Calif.	10,000
Buckeye Open, Toledo, Ohio	60,000	Dick Weber, St. Louis, Mo.	7,000
Cougar Open, New York, N.Y.	85,000	Earl Anthony, Tacoma, Wash.	10,000 and Cougar
Fair Lanes Open, Washington, D.C.	60,000	Johnny Petraglia, Brooklyn, N.Y.	7,000
Don Carter Classic, New Orleans, La.	60,000	Johnny Petraglia, Brooklyn, N.Y.	7,500
Firestone Tour. of Champs, Akron, Ohio	100,000	Johnny Petraglia, Brooklyn, N.Y.	25,000

	PURSE	WINNER	1ST PLACE MONEY
Bellows-Valvair Open, Anaheim, Calif.	$ 50,000	Gary Madison, San Bernardino, Calif.	$ 6,000
Fresno (Calif.) Open	37,500	Ed Bourdase, Fresno, Calif.	4,000
Seattle (Wash.) Open	35,000	Don Johnson, Akron, Ohio	4,000
Portland (Ore.) Open	35,000	Don Helling, St. Louis, Mo.	4,000
Winston-Salem Open, Redwood City, Calif.	50,000	Don Johnson, Akron, Ohio	6,000
Tucson (Ariz.) Open	40,000	Jim Godman, Hayward, Calif.	4,000
El Paso (Tex.) Open	37,500	J. B. Blaylock, Alamogordo, N. Mex.	4,000
Sertoma Open, Houston, Tex.	35,000	Johnny Petraglia, Fresno, Calif.	4,000
Grand Rapids (Mich.) Open	37,500	Tommy Tuttle, King, N.C.	4,000
Waukegan (Ill.) Open	40,000	Don Johnson, Akron, Ohio	4,000
South Bend (Ind.) Open	40,000	Barry Asher, Santa Monica, Calif.	4,000
Winston-Salem Open, Cranston, R.I.	50,000	Roy Buckley, Columbus, Ohio	6,000
Japan Gold Cup, Tokyo, Japan	20,000	Jack Biondolillo, Houston, Tex.	2,000
PBA National Championship, Paramus, N.J.	85,000	Mike Lemongello, N. Babylon, N.Y.	12,500
Lincoln (Neb.) Open	36,000	Larry Laub, San Francisco, Calif.	4,000
American Airlines Open, St. Louis, Mo.	50,000	Barry Asher, Santa Monica, Calif.	6,000
Mercury Open, Rochester, N.Y.	40,000	Johnny Guenther, Fresno, Calif.	Mercury Marquis
Bellows-Vevair Open, Detroit, Mich.	50,000	Don Johnson, Akron, Ohio	6,000
Brunswick World Open, Chicago, Ill.	85,000	Don Johnson, Akron, Ohio	12,000
Hawaiian Invitational, Honolulu	9,000	Dick Weber, St. Louis, Mo.	2,000

1972 Tournaments

	PURSE	WINNER	1ST PLACE MONEY
BPAA U.S. Open, New York, N.Y.	$100,000	Don Johnson, Akron, Ohio	$10,000
Denver (Colo.) Open	50,000	Don Johnson, Akron, Ohio	6,000

(continued on next page)

	PURSE	WINNER	1ST PLACE MONEY
Showboat Inv't'l, Las Vegas, Nev.	$ 77,777	Gus Lampo, Endicott, N.Y.	$11,111
Don Carter Classic, Los Angeles, Calif.	60,000	Bill Beach, Sharon, Pa.	7,500
Mercury-Cougar Open, San Jose, Calif.	85,000	Gus Lampo, Endicott, N.Y.	10,000 and new car
King Louie Open, Kansas City, Mo.	50,000	Larry Laub, San Francisco, Calif.	6,000
Winston-Salem (N.C.) Classic	80,000	Butch Gearhart, Ft. Lauderdale, Fla.	10,000
Fair Lanes Open, Springfield, Va.	60,000	Bobby Meadows, Endicott, N.Y.	7,000
Ebonite Open, Miami, Fla.	75,000	Nelson Burton, Jr., St. Louis, Mo.	10,000
Buckeye Open, Toledo, Ohio	60,000	Curt Schmidt, Ft. Wayne, Ind.	7,000
Miller High Life Open, Milwaukee, Wis.	80,000	Nelson Burton, Jr. St. Louis, Mo.	12,000
Andy Granatelli's STP Classic, New Orleans, La.	70,000	Don Helling, St. Louis, Mo.	10,000
Firestone Tour. of Champs, Akron, Ohio	125,000	Mike Durbin, Dayton, Ohio	25,000
Seattle (Wash.) Open	35,000	Gary Mage, Seattle, Wash.	4,000
Portland (Ore.) Open	37,500	Earl Anthony, Tacoma, Wash.	4,000
Japan Starlanes Open, Redwood City, Calif.	45,000	Earl Anthony, Tacoma, Wash.	4,000
Fresno (Calif.) Open	37,500	Allie Clarke, Akron, Ohio	4,000
Tucson (Ariz.) Open	40,000	Paul Colwell, Tucson, Ariz.	4,000
Winston-Salem Open, Anaheim, Calif.	50,000	Mike McGrath, El Cerrito, Calif.	6,000
Sertoma Open, Houston, Tex.	37,500	Paul Colwell, Tucson, Ariz.	4,000
Columbia 300 Open, Cranston, R.I.	55,000	Barry Asher, Santa Monica, Calif.	8,000
Bay City (Mich.) Open	37,500	Dick Ritger, Hartford, Wis.	4,000
Waukegan (Ill.) Open	42,000	Nelson Burton, Jr., St. Louis, Mo.	4,000
Grand Rapids (Mich.) Open	40,000	Jim Godman, Hayward, Calif.	4,000
South Bend (Ind.) Open	40,000	Matt Surina, Longview, Wash.	4,000
Bellows-Valvair Open, Painesville, Ohio	50,000	Johnny Petraglia, Brooklyn, N.Y.	6,000

	PURSE	WINNER	1ST PLACE MONEY
Japan Gold Cup, Tokyo, Japan	$ 25,000	Barry Asher, Santa Monica, Calif.	$ 2,000
Bellows-Valvair Open, Detroit, Mich.	50,000	Roy Buckley, Columbus, Ohio	6,000
American Airlines Open St. Louis, Mo.	50,000	Earl Anthony, Tacoma, Wash.	6,000
Brunswick World Open, Chicago, Ill.	85,000	Don Johnson, Akron, Ohio	12,000
PBA Nat'l Championship Rochester, N.Y.	65,000	Johnny Guenther, Fresno, Calif.	7,500
Winston-Salem Invitational Honolulu	35,000	Mike McGrath, El Cerrito, Calif.	3,050

(See pages 220–224 for 1973, 1974, and 1975 champions.)

PRO SCORING RECORDS

SIX GAMES—1585, Barry Asher, Costa Mesa, Calif. (South Bend, 1971).

EIGHT GAMES—2139, Ron Lisher, Burlingame, Calif. (San Jose, 1969).

TWELVE GAMES—3048, Roy Buckley, Columbus, Ohio (Chagrin Falls, 1971).

SIXTEEN GAMES—4006, Mike Durbin, Chagrin Falls, Ohio (Akron, 1972).

EIGHTEEN GAMES—4457, Don Johnson, Akron, Ohio (South Bend, 1971).

FORTY-TWO GAMES—10,380, Barry Asher, Costa Mesa, Calif. (South Bend, 1971).

FORTY-TWO GAMES (with bonus pins)—10,755, Barry Asher, Costa Mesa, Calif. (South Bend, 1971).

HIGH SCORE FOR 24th QUALIFIER (18 games)—4179, Ralph Hartmann, New Hyde Park, N.Y. (South Bend, 1971).

MOST 200s IN SUCCESSION—42, Earl Anthony, Tacoma, Wash. (Houston, 1971).

MOST 300s IN TOURNAMENT (Individual—3, Dick Weber, St. Louis (Houston, 1966); Roy Buckley, Columbus, Ohio (Chagrin Falls, 1971).

MOST 300s IN TOURNAMENT—(Aggregate)—11 (South Bend, 1971).

MOST 300s IN ONE SEASON—46 in 1972.

MOST TITLES IN ONE SEASON—7 (1969), Billy Hardwick, Louisville, Ky. (includes All-Star).

MOST TITLES LIFETIME—24, Dick Weber, St. Louis, Mo.; Don Johnson, Las Vegas, Nev.

HIGH AVERAGE FOR 42-GAME TOURNAMENT—247, Barry Asher, Costa Mesa, Calif. (South Bend, 1971).

BEST MATCH GAME RECORD (16 game format)—16 victories, no defeats, Mike McGrath, El Cerrito, Calif. (Paramus, 1969).

BEST MATCH GAME RECORD (24-game format)—22 victories, 2 defeats, George Pappas, Charlotte, N.C. (Kansas City, 1974).

HIGHEST SINGLE MATCH—Bud Horn, Cincinnati, 300, Gary Dickinson, Ft. Worth, Texas, 289 (South Bend, 1971).

OFFICIAL EARNINGS ONE YEAR—$99,585, Earl Anthony, Tacoma (1974).

OFFICIAL EARNINGS LIFETIME—$498,466, Dick Weber, St. Louis (17 years).

THREE-GAME HIGH ON NATIONAL TV—807 (265-266-276). Skee Foremsky, Houston, Texas (Las Vegas, 1969).

(continued on next page)

PRO SCORING RECORDS (cont.)

FOUR-GAME HIGH ON NATIONAL TV—1021 (270-280-233-238), Larry Laub, San Francisco, Calif. (Kansas City, 1972).

HIGHEST SINGLE GAME MATCH ON NATIONAL TV—Don Johnson, Akron, Ohio (299), Dick Ritger, Hartford, Wisc. (268), (Akron, 1970).

PERFECT GAMES ON NATIONAL TV—Jack Biondolillo, Houston, Texas (Akron, 1967); Johnny Guenther, Seattle, Wash. (San Jose, 1969); Jim Stefanich, Joliet, Ill. (Alameda, Calif., 1974).

AMERICAN BOWLING CONGRESS HALL OF FAME
Roster of the Greats

CHARTER MEMBERS 1941
Joseph Bodis, Cleveland
Adolph Carlson, Chicago
Charley Daw, Milwaukee
John Koster, Nyack, N.Y.
Herbert Lange, Watertown, Wis.
Mort Lindsey, Stamford, Conn.
Hank Marino, Milwaukee
James Smith, Buffalo
Harry Steers, Chicago
Gilbert Zunker, Milwaukee

1951
Joseph Wilman, Chicago

1952
Ned Day, Milwaukee

1953
James Blouin, Chicago, Ill.

1954
Joseph Norris, Chicago
William Knox, Philadelphia

1955
James McMahon, Fair Lawn, N.J.

1957
Andy Varipapa, Hempstead, N.Y.

1958
Frank Benkovic, Milwaukee

1959
Walter Ward, Cleveland
George Young, Detroit

1960
Albert Brandt, Lockport, N.Y.

1961
William Sixty, Milwaukee
Phil Wolf, Chicago
  (veterans committee selection)

1962
John Crimmins, Detroit

1963
E. D. Easter, Winston-Salem, N.C.
  (veterans committee selection)
Basil Fazio, Detroit
Steve Nagy, Detroit

1964
Nelson Burton, Sr., St. Louis

1965
Therman Gibson, Detroit

1966
Herbert (Buddy) Bomar, Chicago

1967
Fred Bujack, Sacramento, Calif.
Frank Kartheiser, Chicago
  (veterans committee selection)
Walter (Skang) Mercurio, Cleveland
  (veterans committee selection)

1968
William Bunetta, Fresno, Calif.
Louis Campi, Dumont, N.J.
Alfred Faragalli, Wayne, N.J.
Russell Gersonde, Milwaukee
Edward Kawolics, Chicago
Joseph Kristof, Columbus, Ohio
Paul Krumske, Chicago
Charles O'Donnell, St. Louis
Conrad Schwoegler, Madison, Wis.
Louis Sielaff, Detroit
Tony Sparando, New York
Barney Spinella, Los Angeles

1969
Joe Joseph, Lansing, Mich.
John Martino, Syracuse, N.Y.
  (veterans committee selection)

1970
Donald Carter, Los Angeles
Richard Weber, St. Louis

1971
Edward Lubanski, Detroit
Otto Stein, Jr., St. Louis
   (veterans committee selection)
Frank Thoma, Chicago
   (veterans committee selection)

1972
William Lillard, Houston, Texas
Martin Cassio, Rahway, N.J.
   (veterans committee selection)

Meritorious Service

1963
Peter Howley, Chicago
Elmer H. Baumgarten, Milwaukee
Abraham L. Langtry, Milwaukee
Louis P. Petersen, Chicago
Jack Hagerty, Toledo
Charles O. Collier, Chicago

1966
Harold Allen, Detroit

1968
William Doehrman, Ft. Wayne, Ind.
Cornelius (Cone) Hermann, St. Louis

1969
R. F. Bensinger, Chicago
David A. Luby, Chicago

1973
Ray Bluth, St. Louis, Mo.
Edward Krems, Chicago, Ill.
   (veterans committee selection)

1974
Richard Hoover, Akron, Ohio
Claude (Pat) Patterson, St. Louis
   (veterans committee selection)

1975
William Welu, Houston, Texas
Joseph Falcaro, New York, N.Y.

1970
Samuel Weinstein, Chicago

1971
Howard W. McCullough, Chicago
Sam Levine, Cleveland

1972
LeRoy Chase, Peoria, Ill.
Milton Raymer, Chicago, Ill.

1973
Walt Ditzen, Phoenix, Ariz.

1974
Dennis J. Sweeney, St. Louis, Mo.
Joseph Morton Luby, Sr., Chicago

1975
Frank K. Baker, Milwaukee, Wis.
Vern Eli Whitney, Milwaukee, Wis.

PBA TOURNAMENT MONEY WINNERS THROUGH THE YEARS
1959—Three Tournaments
(Includes All-Star, Masters, World's Invitational)

POS.	BOWLER	AMOUNT	POS.	BOWLER	AMOUNT
1.	Dick Weber	$ 7,672	16.	Dick Hoover	$1,635
2.	Ray Bluth	7,460	17.	Al Savas	1,415
3.	Don Carter	7,085	18.	Carmen Salvino	1,190
4.	Billy Welu	6,892	19.	Joe Donato	1,050
5.	Lou Campi	5,575	20.	Don Ellis	1,011
6.	Billy Golembiewski	5,300	21.	Charlie Wilkinson	860
7.	Ed Lubanski	4,216	22.	Bob Strampe	835
8.	Joe Joseph	3,665	23.	Steve Nagy	685
9.	Harry Smith	3,160	24.	Larry Cassera	600
10.	Tom Hennessey	2,945	25.	John Nickell	600
11.	George Howard	2,502	26.	Bob Chase	600
12.	Buzz Fazio	1,982	27.	Stan Gifford	575
13.	Therm Gibson	1,782	28.	Skip Vigars	550
14.	Bill Bunetta	1,772	29.	Lindy Faragalli	450
15.	Bill Lillard	1,694	30.	Jerry Back	450

(continued on next page)

PBA TOURNAMENT MONEY WINNERS THROUGH THE YEARS (cont.)

POS.	BOWLER	AMOUNT	POS.	BOWLER	AMOUNT
31.	Ralph Engan	$ 425	42.	Johnny Walther	$ 325
32.	Vince Lucci	407	43.	Jim Carman	305
33.	Glenn Allison	400	44.	Bob Crawford	297
34.	Pat Patterson	378	45.	Clyde Hobbs	270
35.	Woody Hulsey	375	46.	Joe Ostroski	250
36.	Bill Pace	364	47.	Johnny King	250
37.	Carl Richard	364	48.	Monroe Moore	250
38.	Morrie Oppenheim	359	49.	Earl Johnson	247
39.	Punk Limmer	350	50.	Bud Hodgson	235
40.	Frank Clause	340	51.	Sam Coleman	235
41.	Tony Lindemann	325			

1960—Seven Tournaments
(Includes All-Star, Masters, World's Invitational)

POS.	BOWLER	AMOUNT	POS.	BOWLER	AMOUNT
1.	Don Carter	$22,525	26.	Jack Biondolillo	$ 2,182
2.	Harry Smith	17,322	27.	Buzz Fazio	2,125
3.	Tom Hennessey	9,248	28.	Jack Lang	2,080
4.	Bob Chase	7,780	29.	Pat Patterson	2,030
5.	Steve Nagy	6,800	30.	Roy Lown	1,975
6.	Dick Weber	6,535	31.	Don Ellis	1,940
7.	Joe Joseph	6,045	32.	Vern Downing	1,905
8.	Ray Bluth	5,585	33.	Bill Pace	1,872
9.	Billy Golembiewski	5,580	34.	Bill Lillard	1,835
10.	Bill Bunetta	5,575	35.	Fred Lening	1,815
11.	Earl Johnson	5,560	36.	Carmen Salvino	1,785
12.	Billy Welu	5,190	37.	Al Savas	1,645
13.	Glenn Allison	4,906	38.	Andy Marzich	1,630
14.	Ed Lubanski	4,610	39.	Ed Shuler	1,600
15.	Morrie Oppenheim	4,395	40.	George Howard	1,458
16.	Ronnie Gaudern	4,100	41.	Lee Jouglard	1,300
17.	Clyde Hobbs	3,266	42.	Red Elkins	1,275
18.	John King	3,129	43.	Joe Donato	1,245
19.	Bob Strampe	3,115	44.	Dick Downey	1,155
20.	Dick Hoover	2,920	45.	Ralph Engan	1,130
21.	Glen Blakesley	2,826	46.	Jim St. John	1,105
22.	Bob Kwolek	2,435	47.	Bob Hitt	1,100
23.	Therm Gibson	2,198	48.	Buddy Bomar	1,060
24.	Stan Marchut	2,196	49.	Ron Diamond	934
25.	J. B. Solomon	2,190	50.	Bud Hodgson	880

1961—Eleven Tournaments
(Includes All-Star, Masters, World's Invitational)

POS.	BOWLER	AMOUNT	POS.	BOWLER	AMOUNT
1.	Dick Weber	$26,280	4.	Roy Lown	$15,491
2.	Ray Bluth	20,827	5.	Bill Tucker	15,297
3.	Don Carter	19,096	6.	Glenn Allison	10,150

POS.	BOWLER	AMOUNT	POS.	BOWLER	AMOUNT
7.	George Howard	$ 9,190	29.	Don Ellis	$ 2,998
8.	Billy Welu	9,100	30.	Steve Nagy	2,419
9.	Rich Robinette	9,061	31.	Tony Lindemann	2,415
10.	Harry Smith	8,777	32.	Don Bickford	2,280
11.	Pat Patterson	8,490	33.	Joe Kristof	2,275
12.	Dick Hoover	8,386	34.	Leo Mann	2,260
13.	Ed Bourdase	8,240	35.	Lewis Ray	2,150
14.	Joe Joseph	7,732	36.	J. B. Solomon	2,148
15.	Dave Soutar	6,480	37.	Bob Chase	2,140
16.	Earl Johnson	6,040	38.	Harold Zinnerman	2,000
17.	Carmen Salvino	5,460	39.	Andy Marzich	1,995
18.	Billy Pace	5,205	40.	Ralph Engan	1,966
19.	Billy Golembiewski	5,040	41.	Bob Kwolek	1,950
20.	Morrie Oppenheim	4,540	42.	Andy Rogoznica	1,860
21.	Vern Downing	4,532	43.	Buzz Fazio	1,835
22.	Ed Lubanski	4,089	44.	Carl Richard	1,817
23.	Dale Seavoy	4,045	45.	John King	1,815
24.	Tom Hennessey	3,807	46.	Luke Barlow	1,800
25.	Jim St. John	3,767	47.	Joe Jacques	1,750
26.	Joe Ostroski	3,675	48.	Dennis Chapis	1,700
27.	Ron Gaudern	3,590	49.	Don Glinski	1,700
28.	Fred Lening	3,026	50.	Tom Harnisch	1,686

1962—Thirty-Two Tournaments
(Includes All-Star, Masters, World's Invitational)

POS.	BOWLER	AMOUNT	POS.	BOWLER	AMOUNT
1.	Don Carter	$49,972	23.	Jim St. John	$ 9,867
2.	Dick Weber	31,320	24.	Skip Vigars	9,655
3.	Joe Joseph	27,100	25.	Fred Lening	9,645
4.	Harry Smith	26,897	26.	Pat Patterson	9,180
5.	Ray Bluth	25,162	27.	Andy Rogoznica	8,557
6.	Glenn Allison	21,910	28.	Bill Pace	8,165
7.	Carmen Salvino	21,425	29.	Ed Bourdase	7,660
8.	Billy Golembiewski	21,115	30.	Richard Downey	7,565
9.	Dick Hoover	20,072	31.	Ronnie Gaudern	7,505
10.	George Howard	18,825	32.	Jim Schroeder	7,327
11.	Tom Hennessey	18,377	33.	Don Bickford	7,140
12.	Al Savas	17,545	34.	Vince Lucci	6,550
13.	Billy Welu	16,042	35.	Bob Crawford	6,350
14.	Dick Agee	15,375	36.	Dennis Chapis	6,280
15.	Glen Blakesley	14,295	37.	J. B. Solomon	6,240
16.	Roy Lown	13,310	38.	Joe Donato	6,065
17.	Andy Marzich	13,222	39.	J. Wilbert Sims	6,045
18.	Bob Strampe	11,430	40.	Bob Kwolek	6,010
19.	Bill Bunetta	10,890	41.	Dave Soutar	5,690
20.	Earl Johnson	10,840	42.	Bob Chase	5,517
21.	Ray Orf	10,100	43.	Darylee Cox	5,395
22.	Ed Lubanski	10,037	44.	Don Ellis	5,070

(continued on next page)

POS.	BOWLER	AMOUNT	POS.	BOWLER	AMOUNT
45.	Vern Downing	$ 4,940	48.	Morrie Oppenheim	$ 4,290
46.	Ron Winger	4,775	49.	John King	4,277
47.	Buzz Fazio	4,387	50.	Jack Henry	4,240

1963—Thirty-Eight Tournaments
(Includes All-Star, Masters, World's Invitational)

POS.	BOWLER	AMOUNT	POS.	BOWLER	AMOUNT
1.	Dick Weber	$46,333	26.	J. B. Blaylock	$ 8,740
2.	Harry Smith	36,962	27.	Bob Strampe	8,072
3.	Jim St. John	35,740	28.	Billy Golembiewski	8,005
4.	Billy Hardwick	33,265	29.	Dennis Chapis	7,840
5.	Billy Welu	31,992	30.	Dick Hoover	7,620
6.	Andy Marzich	30,178	31.	Ed Lubanski	7,597
7.	Earl Johnson	26,332	32.	Monroe Moore	7,537
8.	Ray Bluth	25,625	33.	Don Ellis	7,457
9.	Don Carter	24,140	34.	Fred Lening	7,270
10.	Jack Biondolillo	21,187	35.	Ev Collins	6,905
11.	Bill Allen	19,357	36.	Al Savas	6,900
12.	Glenn Allison	18,007	37.	Buzz Fazio	6,700
13.	Bill Johnson	17,605	38.	Pat Patterson	6,515
14.	Ed Bourdase	17,390	39.	Jim Schroeder	6,402
15.	George Howard	15,300	40.	Lewis Ray	6,180
16.	Wayne Zahn	14,395	41.	Andy Rogoznica	6,117
17.	Vern Downing	14,195	42.	Ted Hoffman	6,050
18.	Les Schissler	14,145	43.	Ray Koehler	5,925
19.	Roger Helle	13,620	44.	Jack Henry	5,685
20.	Bill Bunetta	13,185	45.	Charlie Wilkinson	5,415
21.	Johnny Meyer, Jr.	11,465	46.	Tom Harnisch	5,315
22.	J. B. Solomon	11,265	47.	Joe Joseph	5,220
23.	Carmen Salvino	10,062	48.	Don Winger	5,165
24.	Bob Kwolek	9,942	49.	Darylee Cox	5,095
25.	Tom Hennessey	8,800	50.	Jerry Hale	5,075

1964—Thirty-One Tournaments
(Includes All-Star, Masters)

POS.	BOWLER	AMOUNT	POS.	BOWLER	AMOUNT
1.	Bob Strampe	$33,592	11.	Glenn Allison	$17,985
2.	Bill Allen	29,188	12.	Ed Bourdase	17,427
3.	Billy Hardwick	28,407	13.	Jerry McCoy	17,135
4.	Harry Smith	27,367	14.	Wayne Zahn	16,715
5.	Dick Weber	23,170	15.	Billy Welu	16,150
6.	Ray Bluth	21,205	16.	Johnny King	15,000
7.	Andy Marzich	20,925	17.	Tommy Tuttle	14,885
8.	Jim St. John	18,845	18.	Jack Biondolillo	14,470
9.	Buzz Fazio	18,470	19.	Bill Bunetta	13,920
10.	Carmen Salvino	18,195	20.	Norm Meyers	13,465

POS.	BOWLER	AMOUNT	POS.	BOWLER	AMOUNT
21.	Pete Tountas	$12,995	36.	J. B. Blaylock	$ 7,227
22.	Don Carter	12,312	37.	Tom Hennessey	6,985
23.	Bud Horn	11,575	38.	Tom Harnisch	6,870
24.	Dave Davis	10,235	39.	Gene Rhoda	6,745
25.	Dave Soutar	9,557	40.	Bill Pace	6,630
26.	Don Johnson	9,535	41.	Dennis Taylor	6,495
27.	Jerry Hale	9,490	42.	Sam Baca	6,340
28.	George Howard	8,617	43.	Ted Hoffman	6,335
29.	Eddy Patterson	8,465	44.	Monroe Moore	6,240
30.	Les Schissler	8,367	45.	Billy Golembiewski	6,060
31.	Earl Johnson	7,970	46.	Ralph Brunt	6,057
32.	Ed Lubanski	7,947	47.	Pat Patterson	6,055
33.	Bill Tucker	7,732	48.	Vern Downing	5,995
34.	Mike Lemongello	7,730	49.	Bob Kwolek	5,880
35.	Dick Hoover	7,427	50.	Darylee Cox	5,760

1965—Thirty-Two Tournaments
(Includes All-Star, Masters)

POS.	BOWLER	AMOUNT	POS.	BOWLER	AMOUNT
1.	Dick Weber	$47,675	26.	Skee Foremsky	$12,980
2.	Billy Hardwick	34,518	27.	John Meyer	11,785
3.	Harry Smith	27,107	28.	Ted Hoffman	11,185
4.	Bill Allen	24,995	29.	Don Johnson	11,048
5.	Dave Davis	23,190	30.	Dick Hoover	10,390
6.	Billy Golembiewski	23,095	31.	Eddy Patterson	10,255
7.	Dave Soutar	21,190	32.	Ed Bourdase	10,235
8.	Bob Strampe	21,070	33.	Bud Horn	10,103
9.	Jim St. John	20,697	34.	Jerry Hale	9,540
10.	Jerry McCoy	19,735	35.	Glenn Allison	9,535
11.	Nelson Burton, Jr.	18,525	36.	Joe Joseph	9,400
12.	Ray Bluth	17,842	37.	Fred Lening	9,390
13.	Jack Biondolillo	17,570	38.	Norm Meyers	9,130
14.	Bill Tucker	16,820	39.	Jim Godman	8,300
15	Gene Rhoda	16,300	40.	Al Thompson	7,968
16.	Les Schissler	15,985	41.	Gary Martineau	7,465
17.	Buzz Fazio	15,685	42.	Johnny King	7,267
18.	Mike Lemongello	15,500	43.	John Guenther	7,200
19.	Pete Tountas	14,910	44.	Roy Lown	7,060
20.	Andy Marzich	14,448	45.	Ray Orf	7,050
21.	Billy Welu	14,280	46.	Tom Harnisch	6,788
22.	Carmen Salvino	14,225	47.	Bob Collatos	6,750
23.	Sam Baca	13,605	48.	Ed Lubanski	6,723
24.	Tommy Tuttle	13,478	49.	Wayne Zahn	6,485
25.	Earl Johnson	13,210	50.	Bobby Meadows	6,475

(continued on next page)

1966—Thirty-One Tournaments
(Includes All-Star, Masters)

POS.	BOWLER	AMOUNT	POS.	BOWLER	AMOUNT
1.	Wayne Zahn	$54,720	26.	Fred Lening	$11,275
2.	Dick Weber	50,605	27.	Al Thompson	10,375
3.	Dave Davis	29,115	28.	Roy Lown	10,367
4.	Bob Strampe	23,750	29.	Mike Lemongello	10,195
5.	Nelson Burton, Jr.	23,230	30.	Larry Laub	10,157
6.	Les Schissler	21,940	31.	Carmen Salvino	10,145
7.	John Guenther	20,097	32.	Ed Bourdase	9,960
8.	Dave Soutar	18,885	33.	Tom Harnisch	9,580
9.	Gene Rhoda	18,692	34.	Barry Asher	8,880
10.	Don Johnson	17,605	35.	Jack Biondolillo	8,805
11.	Bobby Jacks	17,435	36.	Earl Johnson	8,760
12.	Pete Tountas	17,015	37.	Billy Hardwick	8,420
13.	Bill Lillard	16,690	38.	Billy Welu	8,335
14.	Harry Smith	16,610	39.	Billy Golembiewski	8,330
15.	Bud Horn	15,255	40.	Bob Collatos	7,702
16.	Bill Tucker	14,985	41.	John Petraglia	7,600
17.	Jim St. John	14,875	42.	Tommy Tuttle	7,240
18.	Jim Godman	14,675	43.	Joe Joseph	7,065
19.	Skee Foremsky	14,615	44.	Jim Dunston	6,725
20.	Bill Allen	14,575	45.	Mike McGrath	6,600
21.	Jim Stefanich	14,510	46.	Bobby Cooper	6,425
22.	Dick Ritger	13,460	47.	Tom Long	6,277
23.	Ted Hoffman	13,405	48.	Dennis Chapis	6,225
24.	Ray Bluth	12,440	49.	George Howard	5,060
25.	Norm Meyers	11,322	50.	Harry O'Neale	5,040

1967—Thirty-Six Tournaments
(Includes All-star, Masters)

POS.	BOWLER	AMOUNT	POS.	BOWLER	AMOUNT
1.	Dave Davis	$54,165	15.	Dick Weber	$20,600
2.	Jim Stefanich	42,575	16.	Bud Horn	19,045
3.	Les Schissler	37,385	17.	Jim Certain	18,540
4.	Don Johnson	32,835	18.	Jim Goodman	17,035
5.	Wayne Zahn	29,380	19.	Bill Tucker	16,997
6.	Carmen Salvino	28,170	20.	John Guenther	16,720
7.	Jack Biondolillo	24,745	21.	Bill Allen	16,281
8.	Jim St. John	24,040	22.	Ted Hoffman	15,905
9.	Skee Foremsky	23,485	23.	Nelson Burton, Jr.	15,821
10.	Mike Durbin	23,035	24.	Tim Harahan	15,390
11.	Bob Strampe	22,486	25.	Tommy Tuttle	15,290
12.	Dave Soutar	22,425	26.	Dick Ritger	14,140
13.	Pete Tountas	22,107	27.	Butch Gearhart	13,965
14.	Billy Hardwick	21,090	28.	Sam Baca	13,595

POS.	BOWLER	AMOUNT	POS.	BOWLER	AMOUNT
29.	Jim Mack	$13,495	40.	Bill Johnson	$ 7,965
30.	Mike Lemongello	12,885	41.	Steve Buell	7,815
31.	Harry Smith	12,720	42.	Billy Golembiewski	7,797
32.	Gene Rhoda	12,045	43.	Bobby Cooper	7,700
33.	Curt Schmidt	11,605	44.	Joe Joseph	7,100
34.	Ralph Engan	10,675	45.	Bill Lillard	6,830
35.	Bob Knipple	10,582	46.	Lou Scalia	6,675
36.	Don Glover	10,445	47.	George Howard	6,400
37.	Billy Welu	10,200	48.	Ed Bourdase	6,120
38.	Norm Meyers	8,670	49.	Glenn Allison	5,930
39.	Mike McGrath	8,095	50.	Buzz Fazio	5,685

1968—Thirty-Six Tournaments
(Includes All-Star, Masters)

POS.	BOWLER	AMOUNT	POS.	BOWLER	AMOUNT
1.	Jim Stefanich	$67,375	26.	Bill Tucker	$13,727
2.	Dave Davis	46,350	27.	Joe Joseph	13,367
3.	Bill Allen	42,125	28.	Norm Meyers	13,130
4.	Don Johnson	38,990	29.	Les Schissler	12,855
5.	Wayne Zahn	38,067	30.	Fred Lening	12,392
6.	Billy Hardwick	35,455	31.	Carmen Salvino	12,337
7.	Dick Ritger	29,432	32.	Ray Bluth	12,030
8.	Nelson Burton, Jr.	28,552	33.	Buzz Fazio	11,817
9.	Dave Soutar	28,475	34.	Pete Tountas	11,590
10.	John Guenther	25,892	35.	Jim Certain	11,580
11.	Don Glover	23,710	36.	Bobby Cooper	10,845
12.	Tim Harahan	22,042	37.	Dick Battista	10,553
13.	Jim Godman	21,125	38.	Tommy Tuttle	9,823
14.	Don Helling	19,317	39.	Jim Mack	9,537
15.	Dick Weber	19,172	40.	Jim St. John	9,350
16.	Ralph Engan	18,867	41.	Bob Knipple	9,295
17.	Skee Foremsky	18,460	42.	Don Carter	9,239
18.	Bob Strampe	18,432	43.	Wally Wagner	9,155
19.	M. Lemongello	18,305	44.	Geo. McDonald	9,035
20.	Teata Semiz	17,825	45.	Vern Downing	8,707
21.	Don McCune	16,645	46.	Glenn Allison	8,660
22.	Mike Durbin	16,450	47.	Gene Rhoda	8,240
23.	Ed Bourdase	16,145	48.	Keith Wiltse	7,967
24.	Harry Smith	15,130	49.	Allie Clarke	7,870
25.	Bud Horn	14,177	50.	Mike McGrath	7,580

1969—Thirty-Five Tournaments
(Includes All-Star, Masters)

POS.	BOWLER	AMOUNT	POS.	BOWLER	AMOUNT
1.	Billy Hardwick	$64,160	4.	Dick Ritger	$38,343
2.	Jim Godman	44,848	5.	Jim Stefanich	37,183
3.	Dick Weber	42,835	6.	Dave Soutar	36,910

(continued on next page)

POS.	BOWLER	AMOUNT	POS.	BOWLER	AMOUNT
7.	Don Johnson	$35,303	29.	Larry Lichstein	$12,720
8.	John Guenther	34,498	30.	Barry Asher	12,635
9.	Don Glover	30,685	31.	Dick Battista	12,593
10.	Mike McGrath	28,650	32.	Carmen Salvino	13,053
11.	Wayne Zahn	24,855	33.	Norm Meyers	11,973
12.	Ralph Engan	24,195	34.	Don Helling	11,965
13.	Bill Allen	22,365	35.	Dale Seavoy	11,523
14.	Tommy Tuttle	21,525	36.	Jim Mack	11,465
15.	Skee Foremsky	20,538	37.	A. W. "Bill" Johnson	11,555
16.	Nelson Burton, Jr.	20,273	38.	Jim St. John	10,795
17.	Dave Davis	20,105	39.	Larry Laub	10,103
18.	Ray Bluth	17,070	40.	Fred Lening	10,030
19.	Tim Harahan	16,593	41.	Pete Tountas	9,870
20.	Allie Clarke	16,255	42.	Ernie Schlegel	9,718
21.	Teata Semiz	16,250	43.	Bud Horn	9,545
22.	Bob Knipple	16,220	44.	Sam Baca	9,293
23.	Butch Gearhart	16,095	45.	Glenn Allison	8,880
24.	Don McCune	15,980	46.	Don Lemon	8,448
25.	Mike Lemongello	14,620	47.	Terry Booth	8,388
26.	Ed Bourdase	13,660	48.	Mike Orlovsky	8,190
27.	Mike Durbin	13,583	49.	Steve Wallace	7,980
28.	John Petraglia	13,233	50.	Vern Downing	7,950

1970—Thirty-Four Tournaments
(Includes All-Star, Masters)

POS.	BOWLER	AMOUNT	POS.	BOWLER	AMOUNT
1.	Mike McGrath	$52,049	21.	Jack Biondolillo	$18,765
2.	Nelson Burton, Jr.	48,950	22.	Dick Weber	18,750
3.	Dave Soutar	46,798	23.	Bob Strampe	18,140
4.	Don Johnson	43,895	24.	Allie Clarke	16,582
5.	Dave Davis	39,460	25.	A. W. "Bill" Johnson	15,595
6.	Jim Stefanich	37,435	26.	Jim Godman	14,925
7.	George Pappas	33,415	27.	Dick Battista	14,920
8.	Skee Foremsky	33,197	28.	Larry Laub	14,827
9.	Dick Ritger	32,102	29.	Tommy Tuttle	13,482
10.	John Petraglia	31,747	30.	Bud Horn	13,400
11.	Earl Anthony	26,200	31.	Gary Mage	12,465
12.	Don Glover	25,445	32.	Larry Lichstein	12,060
13.	Mike Durbin	22,885	33.	Don McCune	11,957
14.	John Guenther	22,112	34.	Don Russell	11,940
15.	Mike Lemongello	21,425	35.	Mike Orlovsky	11,920
16.	Bill Hardwick	21,182	36.	Ralph Engan	9,937
17.	Teata Semiz	20,347	37.	Bob Knipple	9,657
18.	Ed Bourdase	19,895	38.	Alex Seymore	9,590
19.	Bobby Cooper	19,220	39.	Curt Schmidt	9,505
20.	Tim Harahan	19,210	40.	Marty Piraino	9,320

POS.	BOWLER	AMOUNT	POS.	BOWLER	AMOUNT
41.	Roy Buckley	$ 9,307	46.	Bob Sheridan	$ 8,425
42.	Don Helling	9,250	47.	Jim Chestney	8,190
43.	Erie Schlegel	9,042	48.	Keith Wiltse	7,740
44.	Bill Tucker	8,945	49.	Terry Booth	7,545
45.	Jim Mack	8,580	50.	Ralph Hartmann	7,257

1971—Thirty-Four Tournaments
(Includes All-Star, Masters)

POS.	BOWLER	AMOUNT	POS.	BOWLER	AMOUNT
1.	John Petraglia	$85,065	26.	Mike Orlovsky	$17,448
2.	Don Johnson	81,349	27.	Butch Gearhart	17,030
3.	Dave Soutar	43,600	28.	Don McCune	16,990
4.	Mike Lemongello	40,718	29.	Bobby Cooper	16,888
5.	Earl Anthony	40,105	30.	Nelson Burton, Jr.	16,808
6.	Dave H. Davis	38,845	31.	Dick Ritger	15,080
7.	Barry Asher	34,528	32.	Mickey McMahon	14,863
8.	Jim Godman	35,408	33.	Don Glover	14,780
9.	Roy Buckley	33,580	34.	Jim Stefanich	14,170
10.	Dick Weber	31,730	35.	Terry Booth	14,105
11.	Curt Schmidt	26,430	36.	Bob Strampe	13,085
12.	Larry Laub	25,493	37.	Ed Bourdase	12,693
13.	Mike McGrath	25,480	38.	Ernie Schlegel	12,658
14.	John Guenther	24,873	39.	Jim McHugh	12,658
15.	Larry Lichstein	23,593	40.	Norm Meyers	12,390
16.	Dick Battista	22,198	41.	Gus Lampo	12,150
17.	Gary Dickinson	21,835	42.	Tommy Tuttle	12,080
18.	Skee Foremsky	21,143	43.	Don Russell	11,980
19.	Carmen Salvino	19,380	44.	Jack Biondolillo	11,975
20.	Don Helling	18,790	45.	Bud Horn	10,460
21.	Wayne Zahn	18,683	46.	Bill Beach	10,215
22.	Allie Clarke	18,013	47.	Marty Piraino	10,160
23.	Teata Semiz	17,778	48.	Bob Shank	9,313
24.	George Pappas	17,655	49.	Mike Durbin	9,245
25.	Tim Harahan	17,503	50.	Bill Hardwick	8,918

1972   Thirty-Four Tournaments
(Includes All-Star, Masters)

POS.	BOWLER	AMOUNT	POS.	BOWLER	AMOUNT
1.	Don Johnson	$56,648	8.	Roy Buckley	$34,325
2.	Nelson Burton, Jr.	55,930	9.	Bill Beach	33,545
3.	Gus Lampo	40,921	10.	Mike McGrath	32,736
4.	Larry Laub	38,405	11.	Johnny Petraglia	31,933
5.	Curt Schmidt	36,183	12.	Dick Ritger	31,703
6.	Barry Asher	35,123	13.	Jim Godman	30,611
7.	Earl Anthony	34,985	14.	Mike Durbin	29,380

(continued on next page)

POS.	BOWLER	AMOUNT	POS.	BOWLER	AMOUNT
15.	Butch Gearhart	$28,492	33.	Don Glover	$16,225
16.	Tim Harahan	28,183	34.	Carmen Salvino	16,135
17.	Gary Dickinson	27,263	35.	Bobby Cooper	14,828
18.	George Pappas	26,823	36.	Ernie Schlegel	14,478
19.	Dick Weber	26,300	37.	Gary Mage	13,925
20.	Don McCune	23,828	38.	Mickey Higham	13,013
21.	Teata Semiz	22,520	39.	Dave H. Davis	12,645
22.	Paul Colwell	21,900	40.	Jay Robinson	12,390
23.	Johnny Guenther	20,938	41.	Mark Roth	12,103
24.	Dave Soutar	20,395	42.	Bill Johnson	11,913
25.	Skee Foremsky	19,420	43.	Marty Piraino	11,855
26.	Jimmy McHugh	18,552	44.	Palmer Fallgren	11,833
27.	Bobby Meadows	18,368	45.	Larry Lichstein	11,408
28.	Jim Stefanich	18,245	46.	Bob Hood	11,345
29.	Allie Clarke	17,900	47.	Rich Bennett	11,025
30.	Don Helling	17,713	48.	Butch Soper	10,995
31.	Norm Meyers	17,208	49.	Matt Surina	10,980
32.	Mike Lemongello	16,690	50.	Sam Flanagan	10,683

(See page 222 for 1973 and 1974 money winners.)

THE GREATEST OF THE GREAT

In 1970 *Bowling* magazine called upon 48 of the most experienced bowling writers in the game to name all-time All-America teams. All had written and observed bowling closely for a minimum of 15 years. Some could draw on experience stretching back almost 60 years. Of the 48 asked to participate, 47 responded. The other one didn't only because he was on an extended overseas trip and hadn't caught up to his mail.

Two teams were selected, one for the bowlers of the the pre-1950 era, and another for the post-1950 years. The midcentury date was selected as a cutoff because it was at about that time that lane dressing finishes and other great changes in the game took place. To be sure, some bowlers spanned both sides of 1950, as did some of the writers. Some writers were asked to choose one team or the other, and a few participated in both selections.

Thirty scribblers participated in the pre-1950 poll, and the leading vote-getter was the then 80-year-old Hank Marino, who in 1950, in another poll, had been chosen the bowler of the half century.

Jimmy Smith, often termed the first bowling professional because his skill was so great that he toured the country giving exhibitions and instructions more than 50 years ago, was second.

Then came the man usually accorded the distinction of the game's greatest stylist, Ned Day.

The articulate, yet down-to-earth Joe Wilman, who made bowling instruction his way of life, was fourth.

Rounding out the first dream team was the one and only Andy Varipapa. To most, Varipapa is the grandfather of the trick shot, the colorful movie maker. Yet the experts knew that beneath the clown exterior was a great competitor, with the record to prove it.

Jimmy Blouin just missed a first-team berth, but led the second team. He was followed by three great giants of the 1930s and 1940s, Joe Norris, Junie McMahon and Buddy Bomar. One of the biggest surprises was the naming of the legendary John "Count" Gengler to the tenth spot. Gengler did very little formal bowling in league or tournament or even organized match-play shooting. In short, he was a "hustler." But his great skill and charm became so famous that he was recognized as one of the greatest by all.

Honorable mention went to Charley Daw, Frank Benkovic, John Crimmins, Joe Falcaro and Mort Lindsey.

Of the 15, all but Gengler and Falcaro are in the Hall of Fame.

Forty-seven writers took part in the post-1950 pickings. And Don Carter and Dick Weber were unanimous choices. Then came the up-and-down sensasation Billy Hardwick. Probably the most colorful performer of his time, Steve Nagy, also knew what to do with a bowling ball as his record revealed, and was the fourth choice. Rounding out the top five was Eddie Lubanski, who will probably always be remembered as the last of the great two-finger bowlers.

The second team showed Jim Stefanich, Bill Lillard, Ray Bluth, Bob Strampe and Buzz Fazio.

Honorable mention went to Harry Smith, Billy Welu, Joe Wilman, Wayne Zahn, Dick Hoover, Dave Davis, Junie McMahon, Don Johnson, Therm Gibson and George Young.

Of the post-1950 superstars Carter, Weber, Nagy, Lubanski, Lillard, Fazio, Wilman, McMahon, Gibson and Young are already in the Hall of Fame.

Of the top 20 vote-getters, 12 are still top-notch stars and compete regularly on the tour.

In the same election the writers were asked to name the man they considered the greatest bowler of all time.

The nod went to Don Carter with 18 votes. Fourteen selected Hank Marino and 12 picked Dick Weber. Single votes went to Count Gengler, Andy Varipapa and Joe Norris.

The all-time All-America teams point up that a bowler can go for many years. A bowler can be an all-time great, a Hall of Famer, and still be competing in the best competition. This is true in no other sport.

ALL-TIME ALL-AMERICA TEAMS
Selected for the 75th Anniversary issue
of Bowling magazine in 1970 by veteran writers

Pre-1950

1ST TEAM	1ST	2ND	POINTS
Hank Marino, Milwaukee, Wis.	27	1	82
Jimmy Smith, Buffalo, N.Y.	21	6	69
Ned Day, Milwaukee, Wis.	19	8	65
Joe Wilman, Chicago, Ill.	16	8	54
Andy Varipapa, New York	14	6	48

2ND TEAM	1ST	2ND	POINTS
Jimmy Blouin, Chicago, Ill.	14	5	47
Joe Norris, Detroit-Chicago	12	7	43
June McMahon, New York-Chicago	4	9	21
Buddy Bomar, Chicago, Ill.	2	11	17
Count Gengler, New York, N.Y.	4	4	16

HONORABLE MENTION

Votes and points in parenthesis:
Charles Daw, Milwaukee, Wis. (3-3-15) and Frank Benkovic, Milwaukee, Wis. (1-12-15); John Crimmins, Detroit, Mich. (2-8-14); Joe Falcaro, New York, N.Y. (3-2-11); Mort Lindsey, Stamford, Conn. (2-4-10).

Post-1950

1ST TEAM	1ST	2ND	POINTS
Don Carter, St. Louis, Mo.	47	0	141
Dick Weber, St. Louis, Mo.	47	0	141
Billy Hardwick, Louisville, Ky.	25	14	89
Steve Nagy, Cleve-Det-St. L.	17	10	61
Eddie Lubanski, Detroit	14	15	57

2ND TEAM	1ST	2ND	POINTS
Jim Stefanich, Joliet, Ill.	11	17	50
Bill Lillard, Det-Chi-St. L.	10	16	46
Ray Bluth, St. Louis, Mo.	9	10	37
Bob Strampe, Detroit, Mich.	6	19	37
Buzz Fazio, Detroit-St. Louis	7	12	33

HONORABLE MENTION

Harry Smith, Cleve.-Det.-St. Louis (6-13-31); Billy Welu, Houston-St. Louis (6-10-48); Joe Wilman, Chicago (8-0-24); Wayne Zahn, Milwaukee-Atlanta, Tempe, Ariz (3-7-16); Dick Hoover, Akron-St. Louis (1-13-16); Dave Davis, Tucson-Miami (2-9-15); Junie McMahon, New York-Chicago (3-4-13); Don Johnson, Kokomo, Ind., Akron Ohio (3-3-12); Therman Gibson, Detroit (2-4-10); George Young, Detroit (3-1-10).

ALL-TIME LEADING MONEY WINNERS THROUGH OCT. 1, 1975

1. Dick Weber, St. Louis, Mo.	$498,466
2. Don Johnson, Akron, Ohio	421,149
3. Dave Davis, Atlanta, Ga.	377,953
4. Earl Anthony, Tacoma, Wash.	341,303
5. Jim Stefanich, Joliet, Ill.	339,671

PROFESSIONAL BOWLERS ASSOCIATION HALL OF FAME
Established 1974

CHARTER MEMBERS

Don Carter, St. Louis, Mo.
Ray Bluth, St. Louis, Mo.
Carmen Salvino, Chicago, Ill.
Harry Smith, Rochester, N.Y.
Dick Weber, St. Louis, Mo.
Billy Welu, Houston, Texas

MERITORIOUS SERVICE

Frank Esposito, Paramus, N. J.
Chuck Pezzano, Clifton, N. J.

Biographies of Professional Bowlers

EARL ANTHONY

Earl Anthony was a late starter in bowling; he didn't roll a ball until he was 21 and didn't become a full-time pro until he was past 30. But he had a fine athletic career behind him and wasn't about to stay in bowling unless he could do it well. Few in the history of the game have done better than the soft-spoken, crew-cut lefty from Tacoma.

His consistency has amazed his fellow pros and spectators alike. In 1973 he set a record, averaging better than 215 for more than 1,000 games on varying lane conditions. They said that mark would stand for a long time. It didn't, because Anthony set a blistering 219 plus pace in 1974. Earl won six major tournaments and $99,585 in prize money, the most ever by a pro bowler in a single year to that date.

He has become somewhat of a legend, winning 13 titles and almost a quarter of a million dollars in less than six years. The men he rolls with and against are putting him in the all-time great class because he has it all —calmness, clutch ability, stamina, and a quiet type of killer instinct.

Anthony is low key all the way, and he's the first to admit it. "I never expect too much, so when I do well it's a special bonus. I like my hair short, not because I have anything against long hair, but this way it's easier for me to take care of and I feel more comfortable."

He has twice been named Washington's athlete of the year and the 1974 Bowler of the Year and does it all despite two bad knees. Born in Tacoma in 1938, he still lives there—when he isn't out on tour. He's got that attribute of all great athletes. He's so good and makes everything look so easy that it almost seems as though he isn't trying.

Anthony most enjoys the summer tour, when he can take his family along, but no matter what the season, he keeps on winning all year round.

BARRY ASHER

Barry Asher came into his own in 1971 when he won a pair of titles and earned $34,528. He was good before then too. In fact there wasn't a time from the age of 10 when he wasn't the subject of headlines in bowling.

Asher averaged 170 when he was 10, better than 180 at 11 and was a 200 plus averager at 14.

As he grew older his handsome face, a 6′ 1″, 175-pound frame adorned by the latest mod styles and an enthusiasm hard to match got him more writeups than his bowling. But he finally broke the barrier that had him tabbed as bowling's Beau Brummell, a good-looking Jewish kid who loved clothes and carried suitcases full for every pro tour stop.

The big year in 1971 matured Asher, though he was only 24 then. In 1972 he went on to another $35,000 year and two more titles. Always sharp as a talker and a thinker, Barry too often lost his cool when bowling. It happens less and less.

Asher's early coaches included the late Sarge Easter, now a member of the Hall of Fame, and Esther Woods, one of the game's finest female instructors.

"By the time I was 15 I thought I knew all there was to know about bowling. When I started bowling as a pro, I began to find out what I didn't know. I'm still learning."

Once you dig beneath that famous Asher smile and look beyond the fancy clothes, you find a young star who is all bowler, and plans nothing else for a long time.

RAY BLUTH

For too much of his long career Ray Bluth was considered the All-American second-place finisher. Everyone seemed to remember that he was second more than 35 times in major competition. Too often overlooked were his more than 25 titles. Also overlooked is the fact that many of his runnerup finishes were scored only because he moved up from fifth or fourth, and not because he dropped from first.

But in early 1973 the Hall of Fame voters didn't overlook the St. Louis great as he was named to the ABC Hall of Fame.

Solid is the word to best describe Bluth, physically at 5' 10" and 190 and in other ways as a businessman or representing various interests of the game.

Bluth has always looked like a football player, which he was in high school, or a fighter. He has the boxing look only because of a childhood injury to his nose.

A student of the game who parlayed his unique peek-a-boo style to stardom, Bluth is a stickler for details in everything he does. For a guy who is best known for second-place finishes, he has quite a record. He averaged 208 plus for 1,271 games in the All-Star, 211 plus for 730 games in World Invitational play. It's nice to be elected to the Hall of Fame while you're still active. Bluth, 45 when elected, boasts five 800 sets, a dozen 300 games, and his earnings are in the same class with Dick Weber and Don Johnson.

His future is secure. He is a bowling proprietor and his hobbies are photography, studying the stock market, and painting.

NELSON BURTON, JR.

Nelson Burton, Jr., was destined to be a bowler. His father, Nelson Burton, Sr., is a member of the Hall of Fame.

A star in his teens, it came as no surprise when young Burton won his first pro crown at 21, and hasn't stopped since. That was in 1964. In 1970 he won four pro crowns and was named Bowler of the Year. His record is outstanding in every area of play, and the odds are that as soon as he is eligible he and his Dad will make the first father-son team in the Hall.

Burton is one of the finest exponents of the so-called gutter shot, the rolling of a ball down the first board of the lane. Burton had an off year (for him) in 1971, winning a mere $17,000, but came back roaring in 1972 to finish runnerup for Bowler of the Year voting. He earned almost $55,000.

"I can't take it easy. I must bowl plenty to keep in shape," says the 5' 11", 155-pounder who looks as though he could step right into a leading role in a Hollywood film. Young Burton flies his own plane and often uses it on tour stops.

He thinks nothing of practicing 30 games a day, often more. His swing and stroke are among the smoothest in the game, and he adjusts well to all conditions.

Among his outstanding achievements are five 800 series, including one three-game blast of 869. He thinks nothing of it. All his life he has been racking up the big numbers.

JIM GODMAN

When Jim Godman was just 19 and a rookie on the pro tour, he was so good and so impressive that he was named Rookie of the Year. That was in 1965, and he hasn't stopped impressing since.

Godman, at 6' and 185 pounds of solid muscle, is probably the strongest bowler in the game, and nicknames such as "Tarzan" and "Animal" seem to fit.

He's at his best when conditions are tough. His style is one that demands strength as he supports the weight of the ball with his arm during a part of his approach, something most bowlers can't do. He can apply tremendous speed to the ball when necessary, and he seems just as fresh at the end of the night as he did in the morning.

Godman, who got his start in bowling on the West Coast before moving to Ohio and then to Florida, is the only man to win the prestige- and money-laden Firestone Tournament of Champions twice, in 1969 and 1973, each time pocketing pro bowling's best first prize check of $25,000.

Though he knows much about the game and its finer points, Godman is an overpowering type of bowler who can often neutralize a lane condition that is causing other bowlers fits.

Godman doesn't talk much, but when he does, people listen. He is among the top ten all-time money winners, and his cashing percentage has always been one of the best. He was one rookie of the year who more than lived up to his promise.

BILLY HARDWICK

Billy Hardwick will go down as one of the greatest bowlers of all time despite the fact that he has had as many ups and downs as an elevator.

As a rookie he went 17 tournaments without cashing for a dime. He refused to give up, went back home, worked on his game, rounded up some backers, moved out on the tour again and won four titles in 1963 at the tender age of 22. In 1964 he added three more and in 1965 captured the Tournament of Champions. He had a bad year in 1966, a so-so year in 1967, a good year in 1968 and then in 1969 exploded again for six titles and almost $65,000 in prize money. In 1970 he had a so-so year and in 1971 and 1972 bad years, winning less than $10,000.

The true test of a champ is when things are going bad, and that's when Hardwick shines. He was Bowler of the Year in 1964 and 1969 and he jokes, "One year I'm Bowler of the Year and a hero. The next year nobody talks to me."

Hardwick has 16 PBA titles and an All-Star to his credit, and his earnings top the $300,000 mark. For many years he has performed with all kinds of pain, from his hands to every other part of his body.

"I take pills from morning until night," laughs Hardwick, "but they keep me going."

Hardwick is one of the best liked among the pros. He's the first to help the newcomers and any other bowler down on his luck. He has the skill and confidence to keep coming back again and again. And that has earned him the respect of his fellow pros.

DON JOHNSON

"I was never very good at anything, even bowling," says Don Johnson. "But I always did have great desire and concentration. There are many pro bowlers who have a better mechanical game than I do, but few if any try as hard."

From 1967 through 1972 pro bowling was all Don Johnson. He won 18 titles and almost $300,000 to put him second in both titles and money to Dick Weber. But Johnson is almost 11 years younger than Weber. He is almost certain to pass Weber in lifetime earnings as the purses keep going up.

Johnson's heroics earned him back-to-back Bowler of the Year honors from the Bowling Writers Association in 1971 and 1972 and similar back-to-back *Sporting News* Player of the Year honors. The latter is voted by the pros.

A native of Kokomo, Indiana, Johnson is a gregarious type who loves people and has all the patience in the world. He and his wife, Mary Ann, fit in with anyone. He gained 20 pounds after his marriage, but at 5' 10" he handles it well and it didn't hurt his bowling a bit.

His ability to project has made him one of the highest earners in sports. Contracts with Columbia Bowling Ball, Johnson's Gold Palm and half a dozen different tie-ins guarantee him more than $100,000 a year. On the lanes he's an aggressive gambler, always ready, willing and able to adjust to whatever conditions he might find.

A first team All-America selection for six straight years, Johnson feels he has a chance to go down in history with the greatest of all time, and works constantly toward that goal. Only time will tell, but he's already filled more than a few pages in the record books.

MIKE LEMONGELLO

From the time he was a kid, Mike Lemongello found he would rather bowl than eat. And many a day he skipped lunch and saved his eating money for bowling.

As a youngster on Long Island he took a fancy to baseball, but a trip to New Jersey to see the pros in action convinced the 5′ 10″, 140-pounder that bowling was the game for him. He won his first pro title in 1965 when he was 20. He also won the first Cougar Open, the first Don Carter Classic and the first U.S. Open.

Over the years he has been one of the most consistent shooters in the game, averaging around the $25,000 mark in winnings even when he makes only a portion of the tournaments.

Lemongello tries to get bowling down to its simplest common denominator. He isn't a nut on bowling balls and often uses someone else's ball because it feels comfortable. On playing lanes he has no deep secrets. "I watch Dave Soutar, whom I consider the best, and follow his line. If Soutar isn't around, I see who is scoring well and use them as a guide."

Mike's whole attitude is one of relaxation, though he admits there is always inner turmoil. He has always been quiet, to the point where some wondered how he could ever woo and win a girl. His lovely wife, Joyce, a former airline hostess, is at his side constantly.

Mike is extremely close to his family, particularly to his brother Pete, a popular singing star. He is well known to all but is most respected by his fellow pros.

He doesn't talk much, but his ball talks strikes and 220 averages all the time.

MIKE McGRATH

Mike McGrath won his first pro crown while still a college student. He didn't drop his studies and has a marketing degree from Chico State in California.

He also has a doctorate in bowling with back-to-back PBA National championships and five other PBA crowns. The slim lefty says he panics when he's on TV, but he has twice come through with clutch doubles in the final frame to cop major titles.

In 1970 as a 24-year-old he won $51,149. He enjoys the tour, takes his family with him as much as possible. He and wife Sandy enjoy taking in the historical sights and mixing as much as possible.

McGrath is outspoken in his opinions, feels that too many bowlers take the game too seriously too much of the time. "The tour is rough physically and mentally, so you've got to take your mind off the game now and then to perform your best."

There has been a lefty-righty controversy from time to time. McGrath feels that left-handed bowlers of his ability don't get as much credit as they deserve. "We should be considered on our merits as bowlers, not as left-handed or right-handed bowlers."

He doesn't feel there are any secrets in the game. "Every bowler knows what he can do, and he should work on the things he can't do too well. It's as simple as that."

McGrath likes to get things down to simple terms. He wants to make money bowling and then use his brain to make more money with the bowling money. So far he's done all right.

JOHN PETRAGLIA

Johnny Petraglia still plays stickball during some of his short stays at home in Brooklyn.

As a kid growing up in Brooklyn his sights were set on a career in baseball or gymnastics. He wasn't quite good enough at either, so then he decided it would be great if he could eke out a living with his bowling ball.

At 17 he was winning tournaments. At 19 he had his first pro triumph. He didn't let a tour with the Green Berets in Viet Nam dim his enthusiasm. His main thoughts, aside from dodging bullets, were to get back and bowl. And bowl he did. His first full year out of service, 1969, just 21, earned him almost $14,000. In 1970 he boosted it to $31,000.

And in 1971 he was the talk of the bowling world as he won five tournaments, appeared on the Pro Bowlers Tour network TV show 8 of 13 weeks and went on to win $85,065, the most ever won by a bowler in a single year.

Superstar bowler John Petraglia isn't much different from stickball player John Petraglia. "I'm doing what I love, and I love what I'm doing. I'm making money, seeing the world, and living the dream I hoped might someday come true."

But the competitive Petraglia is no softie. At 5' 11" and 150, the lithe lefthander doesn't look as strong as he is. He's calm and collected in the clutch, so much a student of the game that many of the pros come to him for advice.

He takes little for granted, continues to work on his game endlessly. "I worked hard to get results. I'll work harder to keep getting them," says John. The results are obvious. Any bowler would gladly settle for one of Petraglia's so-called bad years.

DICK RITGER

Dick Ritger was a late starter as a pro bowler, going full time at 27. It was quite a decision for the Hartford, Wisconsin, kegler who exudes the All-American boy concept.

He was a college grad, secure as the recreation director of his town, and with a growing family when he made the move. It paid off. His first two titles came in 1966. Through 1972 he had captured ten crowns and averaged around $30,000 a year in tournament winnings.

But that's not all. The 5′ 7″, 145-pounder has parlayed his education, his teaching experience, his ability to impart his know-how and his enthusiasm for people into a package bowling always needs, an individual who can conduct a clinic or a seminar, appear on TV, or do almost anything else and present bowling in its greatest image. This all means extra bucks in the Ritger pocket, and if he never rolls another competitive ball, his future in the game is secure.

"As long as I'm capable of winning on the tour, I'll bowl," says Dick. "Once it gets to be a struggle, I'll quit."

A meticulous planner, it's not surprising that he recommends a game plan in bowling. "Deep thinking goes into all sports, but is too often overlooked in bowling. Chart your entire game from start to finish. If something goes wrong, take another look and find where you went wrong."

Ritger has been honored many times by his fellow pros by election to the most important committees. He is sure his role in later life will be to teach bowlers and to teach bowlers how to teach other bowlers.

His pro triumphs, other titles and All-America honors prove that nice guys do finish first.

CARMEN SALVINO

Carmen Salvino was making a living as a pro bowler when he was 17. And that was in 1950, a decade before the PBA was born. He won his first pro title in 1961. And in 1973 he introduced his equation theory to win his eleventh crown.

"There's more to this bowling than meets the eye," says Carmen. "An engineer friend of mine has it down to a science, and it's working." Salvino is another of the all-time greats who have weathered changing conditions by changing their game to suit the conditions.

A health buff, Salvino exercises regularly and carefully, chooses his foods with care, and is always on a strict routine. Known as the "Spook" in his early days because of his devil-may-care antics, he settled down, but still remains one of the most colorful bowlers in the game. He is immensely popular in Japan.

"The fans deserve all you've got, and I try to give it to them anytime I can," says Carmen.

He's been a TV darling and he's always had one or two sponsors to keep him going because he does have a feeling for the people who help pay the bills.

Except for a short stay in the National Bowling League in Dallas, Chicago has been his home all his life. That's where he resided; his second home is the bowling center he happens to be in because he has a family of fans wherever he goes.

TEATA SEMIZ

When Teata Semiz was a kid he earned his extra money by setting up pins. And when business was slow he would set up the pins for himself, then knock them down. It's a tiring way to learn the game, almost like playing tennis against yourself.

In those days the big hook was the vogue and the Jersey youngster learned how to roll a hook. He learned his hook almost too well. It was effective when it hit the 1-3 pocket, but when it didn't it was as wild as the crop of hair Semiz had flying around the top of his head.

He tamed both his hair and his hook. He took a year to develop a so-called line ball, but it worked. As a part-time tourist in the latter 1960s and early 1970s he has averaged $1,000 per tournament in winnings.

Semiz didn't go out on the tour until 1968, when he was 34, an age most athletes see as being over the hill. But Semiz keeps in fine shape as a construction worker on the newly rising skyscrapers in New York City.

"I like my job, and I love to bowl. And I'll do both just as long as I can," says Semiz.

Winner of two pro titles, he also captured the American Bowling Congress singles and all-events in 1972. In 1966 he rolled an 867 series in league play, scoring games of 299, 268 and 300.

Semiz looks rough and tough on the lanes, and he is. Off the lanes he's a softie who spends much of his time coaching his daughter and son in all sports and pampering his collie dogs.

JIM STEFANICH

When ABC-TV wanted to stage a sports superstar spectacular featuring ten athletes competing in sports other than their own, Jim Stefanich was the bowling representative.

He's a fine golfer who probably could have done well as a golf pro, and is always in fine physical shape. He received his first recognition by winning an ABC title and since has won five more for a record; that gave him an opportunity to compete in international competition, and in 1963 and 1964 he captured four firsts, a second and third against the best amateurs in the world.

He did just as well when he jumped into the pro ranks. After winning $15,000 his first full year he zoomed to $42,000 in 1967 and then to $67,000 in 1968 when his all-around play earned him Bowler of the Year honors.

From 1966 through 1972 he earned more than a quarter of a million dollars with his bowling ball. He started bowling in 1957 when he was 16 and quickly became a star in the Joliet, Illinois, area.

Stefanich is smooth, works hard to come out of the ball easily and cleanly, is particularly noted for his TV performances, where he isn't afraid to gamble during the hit-or-miss one-game matches.

In the superstar competition he faced the likes of Joe Frazier, Jean Claude Killy, Bob Seagren, Elvin Hayes, Johnny Unitas, Rod Gilbert, Rod Laver, Peter Revson and Johnny Bench. He finished seventh, but proved to many that bowlers are athletes, at least Jim Stefanich is.

BOB STRAMPE

Bob Strampe is one of the old pros who started in the days when team bowling was the big thing. He went from early fame in Minneapolis to stardom in Detroit, then in the ill-fated National Bowling League and finally on the pro tour.

He was the second bowler to win the grand slam of bowling. Don Carter was the first. Strampe captured the All-Star in 1963, the PBA National in 1964 and the ABC Masters in 1966.

At 5′ 10″ and 160 he looks frail but has always been known to be one of the strongest bowlers in the game, using speed any time he needs it. Strampe was the master of the inside angle, but learned how to adjust to all angles.

In 1971, when he was 40, he was one of 30 persons from various fields honored by Benrus. The watch firm was honoring first-timers, fast-timers and longtimers. Among the award winners were Hank Aaron, Larry Brown, Margaret Smith, Joan Crawford, J. Edgar Hoover, Billy Kidd, Bobby Orr, Bill Shoemaker, Lowell Thomas, Bill Toomey, Lee Trevino and Johnny Unitas.

The longtime feat that earned him his place with those names is his fantastic all-time American Bowling Congress tournament average record of 211 plus for 111 games over a ten-year span.

Strampe, in addition to his bowling prowess, is a fine announcer with a good voice and command of the language. He is witty and humorous.

Asked why he cut his speed, he laughs, "I didn't. I'm rolling harder, but at my age the ball goes slower." According to his opponents, there's been no slowdown in Strampe's ability.

DICK WEBER

For years it seemed Dick Weber had nowhere to go but down. Maybe life does begin at 40 for a guy like Weber, for at just past 40 he had notched the most pro titles, 23, earned more than $400,000 in prize money, set himself up for life with business ventures, and been selected to the highest honor his game can bestow, the ABC Hall of Fame.

"I don't think I'll ever want to quit pro bowling," says the slim St. Louis bowler who most of the time weighs in at less than 140, and has been that way for more than twenty years.

Whenever he's asked about quitting, Weber's reply is the same, "I think I can win a few more years."

Weber's career has spanned the most varying lane conditions the game has known, and he's been a winner on all of them. An All-America selection eleven times and Bowler of the Year three, he is rated in the top three of all-time. He has won more major titles than any other bowler and it's unlikely anyone will ever catch him.

He left Indiana in the early 1950s to seek his fame and fortune in St. Louis, and it's been all up ever since. Weber has always been somber and serious when a championship is at stake, but there is also the sentimental Dick Weber who burst into tears at his Hall of Fame induction and at the completion of his two-year term as president of the PBA.

And there's another promising pro who hits the tour from time to time, Dick Weber, Jr. But Weber, Sr., isn't about to move out; he always has a few more good years.

WAYNE ZAHN

Wayne Zahn seriously considered a career in baseball before he turned to bowling. And at the early stages of his pro career he wondered if he had made the right choice.

The turning point came in 1966. Off a very bad year in 1965, Zahn won the biggest one of them all, the Firestone Tournament of Champions. He went on to win the PBA National the same year, almost $55,000 and Bowler of the Year honors.

At 19 Zahn averaged 222 in Milwaukee and finished ninth in the All-Star. He was the first to admit that he had much to learn in his first attempts at the pro side of the game. But he learned his lessons well. He and roommate Dick Ritger are fine physical specimens who keep working to keep their bodies in top shape.

Zahn's dozen pro crowns, including a second PBA National in 1968, rate him with the tops in the pro ranks, and his all-time earnings rate him in the top ten.

A quiet, unassuming 6-footer, Zahn is a family man who looks on bowling as his business. He also operates a bowling center in Arizona, his current home after a stop at Atlanta.

His big asset in bowling is a great armswing, the kind most pros strive for but seldom achieve. As a youngster he rolled a roundhouse hook; he soon cut it down to one of reasonable size, but Zahn is still more than capable of putting whatever he needs on the ball.

Baseball's loss has been bowling's gain. At a time when he might be all through in baseball, Zahn is still a threat in every event in which he competes.

PBA CHAMPIONS OF 1973 AND 1974

1973 Tournaments

	PURSE	WINNER	1ST PLACE MONEY
San Jose Open, San Jose, Calif.	$ 65,000	Allie Clarke	$ 7,500
Don Carter Classic, Los Angeles, Calif.	70,000	Gary Dickinson	7,500
Showboat Invitational, Las Vegas, Nev.	77,777	Barry Asher	**11,111**
Denver Open, Denver, Col.	50,000	Jay Robinson	6,000
King Louie Open, Kansas City, Mo.	50,000	Bob Knipple	6,000
Lincoln-Mercury Open, New Orleans, La.	85,000	Carmen Salvino	10,000 and new car
Fair Lanes Open, Baltimore, Md.	60,000	Dick Ritger	7,000
Winston-Salem Classic, Winston-Salem, N.C.	90,000	Don McCune	10,000
Miller High Life Open, Milwaukee, Wis.	80,000	Don McCune	12,000
BPAA U.S. Open, New York, N.Y.	75,000	Mike McGrath	7,500
Ebonite Open, Toledo, Ohio	80,000	Dick Weber	10,000
STP Classic, Miami, Fla.	80,000	Dick Ritger	10,000
Firestone Tournament of Champions, Akron, Ohio	125,000	Jim Godman	25,000
Winston-Salem Open, Downey, Calif.	55,000	Don McCune	6,000
Home Box Office Open, Portland, Ore.	47,500	Dave Soutar	5,000
Seattle Open, Seattle, Wash.	35,000	Earl Anthony	4,000
Fresno Open, Fresno, Calif.	37,500	Don McCune	4,000
Redwood City Open, Redwood City, Calif.	40,000	Don McCune	4,000
Home Box Office Open, Tucson, Ariz.	47,500	Barry Asher	5,000
Houston-Sertoma Open, Houston, Tex.	37,500	Don Johnson	4,000
Ft. Worth Open, Ft. Worth, Tex.	37,500	Gary Dickinson	4,000
Home Box Office Open, Pennsville, N.J.	47,500	Mike McGrath	5,000
Starlanes-Ebonite Open, Cranston, R.I.	50,000	Paul Colwell	5,000

	PURSE	WINNER	1ST PLACE MONEY
Bay City Open, Bay City, Mich.	$ 37,500	Don Johnson	$ 4,000
Columbia 300 Open, Waukegan, Ill.	55,000	Marty Piraino	6,000
Home Box Office— PBA Nat. Championship Oklahoma City, Okla.	70,000	Earl Anthony	8,000
Japan Gold Cup, Tokyo, Japan	25,000	Don McCune	2,000
Brunswick Eastern Open, Bayside, N.Y.	50,000	Matt Surina	5,000
Painesville Open, Painesville, Ohio	40,000	Paul Colwell	4,000
Canada Dry Open, Detroit, Mich.	50,000	Dick Ritger	5,000
Brut Open, St. Louis, Mo.	50,000	Butch Gearhart	5,000
Brunswick World Open, Chicago, Ill.	100,000	Jim Godman	14,000
Winston-Salem Invitational Hawaii	35,000	Mike McGrath	3,000

1974 Tournaments

	PURSE	WINNER	1ST PLACE MONEY
Midas Open, Alameda, Calif.	$100,000	Dick Ritger	$14,000
Carter Classic, Arcadia, Calif.	70,000	Larry Laub	7,500
Showboat Classic, Las Vegas, Nev.	100,000	Jim Stefanich	14,000
King Louie Open, Kansas City, Mo.	55,000	George Pappas	6,000
Cleveland Rotary Open, Cleveland, Ohio	60,000	Larry Laub	7,000
Fair Lanes Open, Baltimore, Md.	70,000	Dick Ritger	7,500
BPAA U.S. Open, New York, N.Y.	85,000	Larry Laub	8,000
Winston-Salem Classic, Winston-Salem, N.C.	100,000	Ed Ressler	14,000
STP Classic, Miami, Fla.	80,000	Alex Seymore	10,000
New Orleans Lions Open, New Orleans, La.	55,000	Paul Colwell	6,000
Lincoln Mercury Open, Denver, Col.	85,000	John Guenther	10,000 plus new Cougar car
Miller High Life Open, Milwaukee, Wis.	80,000	John Guenther	10,000

(continued on next page)

PBA CHAMPIONS OF 1973 AND 1974 (cont.)

	PURSE	WINNER	1ST PLACE MONEY
Ebonite Open, Toledo, Ohio	$ 80,000	Wayne Zahn	$10,000
Firestone Tourney of Champions Akron, Ohio	125,000	Earl Anthony	25,000
Los Angeles Open, Los Angeles, Calif.	75,000	Earl Anthony	9,000
Seattle Open, Seattle, Wash.	45,000	Ed Bourdase	5,000
Winston-Salem Open, Portland, Ore.	55,000	Gary Dickinson	6,000
Home Box Office Open, San Jose, Calif.	47,000	Earl Anthony	5,000
Fresno Open, Fresno, Calif.	47,000	Earl Anthony	5,000
Home Box Office Open, Tucson, Ariz.	47,000	Bob Hood	5,000
Houston Sertoma Open, Houston, Tex.	47,000	Tom Hudson	5,000
Home Box Office Open, Hartford, Conn.	50,000	Nelson Burton	5,000
New Jersey Open, Edison, N.J.	50,000	Carmen Salvino	5,000
Home Box Office Open, Buffalo, N.Y.	50,000	Dave Soutar	5,000
Star Lanes Ebonite Open, Waukegan, Ill.	50,000	Dick Ritger	5,000
Canada Dry Open, Detroit, Mich.	55,000	Steve Neff	5,000
Buzz Fazio Open, Battle Creek, Mich.	50,000	Don Johnson	5,000
Canada Dry Open, Cleveland, Ohio	50,000	Earl Anthony	5,000
Columbia 300 Open, Syracuse, N.Y.	50,000	Skee Foremsky	5,000
Brunswick World Open, Chicago, Ill.	100,000	John Petraglia	14,000
Winston-Salem Invitation, Hawaii	35,000	Earl Anthony	3,000

PBA TOURNAMENT MONEY WINNERS OF 1973 AND 1974
1973—Thirty-Four Tournaments
(Includes ABC, Masters)

POS.	BOWLER	AMOUNT	POS.	BOWLER	AMOUNT
1.	Don McCune	$69,000	3.	Jim Godman	$57,808
2.	Barry Asher	58,996	4.	Dick Ritger	55,818

POS.	BOWLER	AMOUNT	POS.	BOWLER	AMOUNT
5.	Earl Anthony	$45,813	28.	John Guenther	$17,858
6.	Don Johnson	41,670	29.	Sam Flanagan	17,828
7.	Carmen Salvino	38,303	30.	Bobbie Knipple	17,788
8.	Gary Dickinson	35,983	31.	Bob Strampe	16,670
9.	Roy Buckley	35,733	32.	John Petraglia	16,635
10.	Jay Robinson	35,615	33.	Allie Clarke	16,475
11.	Mike McGrath	32,838	34.	Don Helling	15,660
12.	Paul Colwell	30,595	35.	Jim McHugh	15,533
13.	Dick Weber	28,215	36.	Steve Neff	14,295
14.	Dennis Swayda	27,778	37.	Mike Lemongello	14,243
15.	Dave Soutar	26,518	38.	Bill Johnson	14,238
16.	Matt Surina	25,815	39.	Skee Foremsky	14,188
17.	Larry Laub	25,790	40.	Butch Soper	13,935
18.	Jim Stefanich	25,100	41.	John Handegard	13,750
19.	Norm Meyers	24,295	42.	Tye Critchlow	13,143
20.	Bobby Cooper	23,525	43.	Butch Gearhart	13,085
21.	Gus Lampo	22,610	44.	Art Trask	12,595
22.	Ernie Schlegel	22,140	45.	Tim Harahan	12,220
23.	George Pappas	22,055	46.	Les Zikes	11,995
24.	Dave Davis	20,610	47.	Lou Moore	11,710
25.	Mark Roth	19,900	48.	Marty Piraino	11,563
26.	Nelson Burton, Jr.	19,813	49.	Alex Saymore	11,385
27.	Teata Semiz	18,024	50.	Mickey Higham	11,363

1974—Thirty Tournaments
(Includes ABC, Masters)

POS.	BOWLER	AMOUNT	POS.	BOWLER	AMOUNT
1.	Earl Anthony	$99,585	23.	George Pappas	$23,357
2.	Larry Laub	63,735	24.	Norm Meyers	22,060
3.	Jim Stefanich	54,410	25.	Teata Semiz	21,750
4.	John Petraglia	52,410	26.	Sam Flanagan	21,532
5.	Dick Ritger	45,235	27.	Bob Hood	21,280
6.	Alex Seymore	37,127	28.	Tim Harahan	20,742
7.	Mark Roth	35,779	29.	Steve Neff	20,676
8.	Dick Weber	35,621	30.	Gary Mage	20,075
9.	Roy Buckley	34,792	31.	Butch Gearhart	19,552
10.	Paul Colwell	34,530	32.	Dave Soutar	19,297
11.	Johnny Guenther	33,580	33.	Skee Foremsky	18,526
12.	Dave Davis	32,280	34.	Barry Asher	16,772
13.	Don McCune	30,857	35.	Jim Godman	16,495
14.	Carmen Salvino	30,316	36.	Les Schissler	15,530
15.	Gary Dickinson	29,887	37.	Dale Glenn	15,457
16.	Ed Ressler	28,400	38.	Mickey Higham	15,332
17.	Wayne Zahn	28,390	39.	Art Trask	14,390
18.	Jay Robinson	28,100	40.	Tom Hudson	14,345
19.	Nelson Burton, Jr.	26,965	41.	Bill Allen	13,610
20.	Don Johnson	25,327	42.	Ed Bourdase	13,005
21.	Curt Schmidt	23,680	43.	Bob Strampe	12,647
22.	Matt Surina	23,590	44.	Joe Berardi	12,526

(continued on next page)

PBA TOURNAMENT MONEY WINNERS OF 1973 AND 1974 (cont.)

POS.	BOWLER	AMOUNT	POS.	BOWLER	AMOUNT
45.	Butch Soper	$12,150	48.	Louie Moore	$11,407
46.	Marty Piraino	11,955	49.	Craig Mueller	11,300
47.	Ernie Schlegel	11,762	50.	Jim Frazier	11,292

PBA CHAMPIONS OF 1975 (THROUGH OCT. 1)

	PURSE	WINNER	1ST PLACE MONEY
ARC Open, Alameda, Calif.	$ 60,000	Barry Asher	$ 7,000
Los Angeles Open, Arcadia, Calif.	60,000	Earl Anthony	7,000
Showboat Invitational, Las Vegas, Nev.	100,000	Carmen Salvino	14,000
Denver Open, Denver, Col.	60,000	Larry Laub	7,000
King Louie Open, Overland Park, Kan.	60,000	Mark Roth	7,000
Copenhagen Open, N. Olmsted, Ohio	85,000	Paul Colwell	7,000
Fair Lanes Open, Springfield, Va.	70,000	Gary Dickinson	7,500
Long Island Open, Garden City, L.I., N.Y.	60,000	Earl Anthony	7,000
Midas Open, Windsor Locks, Conn.	100,000	Nelson Burton, Jr.	14,000
Ebonite Don Carter Classic, Miami, Fla.	70,000	Dick Ritger	7,500
Lincoln-Mercury Open, St. Louis, Mo.	75,000	Ed Ressler	10,000
Monroe Max-Air Open, Metairie, La.	80,000	Don Helling	10,000
BPAA U.S. Open, Grand Prairie, Tex.	100,000	Steve Neff	10,000
Miller High Life Open, Wauwatosa, Wis.	80,000	Dave Davis	10,000
Ebonite Open, Toledo, Ohio	85,000	Louis Moore	10,000
Firestone Tournament of Champions, Akron, Ohio	125,000	Dave Davis	25,000
Brunswick PBA National, Downey, Calif.	75,000	Earl Anthony	9,000
Sacramento Open, Sacramento, Calif.	50,000	Sam Flanagan	6,000

PBA CHAMPIONS OF 1975 (THROUGH OCT. 1) (cont.)

	PURSE	WINNER	1ST PLACE MONEY
Portland Open, Portland, Ore.	50,000	Sal Bongiorno	6,000
Seattle Open, Seattle, Wash.	50,000	John Guenther	6,000
San Jose Open, San Jose, Calif.	50,000	Palmer Fallgren	6,000
Fresno Open, Fresno, Calif.	50,000	Marshall Holman	6,000
Tucson Open, Tucson, Ariz.	50,000	Don Johnson	6,000
Quad Cities Open, Davenport, Iowa	50,000	Earl Anthony	6,000
Home Box Office Open, Pittsburgh, Pa.	50,000	Carmen Salvino	6,000
Jackson Open, Jackson, N.J.	50,000	Earl Anthony	6,000
Home Box Office Open, Buffalo, N.Y.	50,000	Tom Hudson	6,000
Waukegan Open, Waukegan, Ill.	50,000	Earl Anthony	6,000
Columbia 300 Open, Detroit, Mich.	55,000	Dale Glenn	6,000

PBA TOURNAMENT MONEY WINNERS OF 1975 (THROUGH OCT. 1)

POS.	BOWLER	AMOUNT	POS.	BOWLER	AMOUNT
1.	Earl Anthony	$94,615	7.	Mark Roth	$35,862
2.	Dave Davis	50,935	8.	Gary Dickinson	33,326
3.	Carmen Salvino	50,133	9.	Larry Laub	32,138
4.	Ed Ressler	43,553	10.	Steve Neff	31,330
5.	Nelson Burton, Jr.	39,705	11.	Roy Buckley	29,473
6.	Paul Colwell	35,940	12.	Barry Asher	28,175